DEC 1 4 2006

OPPOSING
VIEWPOINTS®
SERIES

Police Brutality

Other Books of Related Interest:

Opposing Viewpoints Series

Civil Liberties

Crime and Criminals

National Security

Race Relations

The War on Terrorism

Current Controversies Series

America's Battle Against Terrorism

Crime

Guns and Violence

At Issue Series

Guns and Crime

Police Corruption

Racial Profiling

"Congress shall make
no law . . . abridging
the freedom of speech,
or of the press."

First Amendment to the U.S. Constitution

The basic foundation of our democracy is the First Amendment guarantee of freedom of expression. The Opposing Viewpoints Series is dedicated to the concept of this basic freedom and the idea that it is more important to practice it than to enshrine it.

OPPOSING
VIEWPOINTS®
SERIES

Police Brutality

Sheila Fitzgerald, Book Editor

GREENHAVEN PRESS
An imprint of Thomson Gale, a part of The Thomson Corporation

THOMSON
—★—™
GALE

Detroit • New York • San Francisco • New Haven, Conn. • Waterville, Maine • London

Christine Nasso, *Publisher*
Elizabeth Des Chenes, *Managing Editor*

© 2007 Thomson Gale, a part of The Thomson Corporation.

Thomson and Star logo are trademarks and Gale and Greenhaven Press are registered trademarks used herein under license.

For more information, contact:
Greenhaven Press
27500 Drake Rd.
Farmington Hills, MI 48331-3535
Or you can visit our Internet site at http://www.gale.com

Cover photograph reproduced by permission of iStockphoto.com/Jackie Oldo.

LIBRARY OF CONGRESS CATALOGING-IN-PUBLICATION DATA

Police brutality / Sheila Fitzgerald, book editor.
    p. cm. -- (Opposing viewpoints)
  Includes bibliographical references and index.
  ISBN-13: 978-0-7377-3358-7 (lib. : alk. paper)
  ISBN-10: 0-7377-3358-6 (lib. : alk. paper)
  ISBN-13: 978-0-7377-3359-4 (pbk. : alk. paper)
  ISBN-10: 0-7377-3359-4 (pbk. : alk. paper)
  1. Police brutality--Juvenile literature. I. Fitzgerald, Sheila.
  HV8141.P565 2006
  363.2'32--dc22
                                                              2006022915

Printed in the United States of America
10 9 8 7 6 5 4 3 2 1

Contents

Why Consider Opposing Viewpoints?   11

Introduction   14

Chapter 1: Is Misconduct in Law Enforcement a Serious Problem?

Chapter Preface   19

1. Police Brutality Is Widespread   21
   U.S. Commission on Civil Rights

2. The Extent of Police Brutality Is Exaggerated   28
   Russell G. Redenbaugh

3. Antiterrorism Policies Result in Police Abuse   34
   of Dissenters
   Heidi Boghosian

4. The War on Terror Has Led to More Use of   46
   Excessive Force
   Llewellyn H. Rockwell Jr.

Periodical Bibliography   51

Chapter 2: What Factors Cause Police Brutality?

Chapter Preface   53

1. Racism Is a Factor in Police Violence   55
   Sundiata Keita Cha-Jua

2. The Police Are Not Racist   63
   Heather Mac Donald

3. The Militarization of Law Enforcement   70
   Causes Police Brutality
   Donald E. Wilkes Jr.

4. Ineffective Handling of the Mentally Ill   **81**
Causes Police Brutality
Adelle Waldman

Periodical Bibliography   **87**

Chapter 3: Does the War on Terror Invite Law-Enforcement Abuses?

Chapter Preface   **89**

1. Delayed-Notice Searches Invite Police Abuses   **91**
Donald E. Wilkes Jr.

2. Delayed-Notice Searches Are Needed to   **99**
Thwart Terrorism
Chuck Rosenberg

3. Police Shoot-to-Kill Policies Invite Abuse of Force   **106**
Tim Hames

4. Police Shoot-to-Kill Policies Are Necessary to   **111**
Stop Suicide Bombers
Emanuele Ottolenghi

Periodical Bibliography   **116**

Chapter 4: How Can Police Misconduct Be Reduced?

Chapter Preface   **118**

1. Racial Profiling Should Be Eliminated   **120**
Nelson Lund

2. Racial Profiling Does Not Contribute to   **127**
Police Misconduct
Heather Mac Donald

3. The Use of Tasers Should Be Suspended   **133**
Amnesty International

4. Tasers Prevent Excessive Force   **139**
Rick Smith

5. Community Policing Reduces Police Brutality   **146**
  Edward A. Flynn

6. Video Monitoring Reduces Police Brutality   **155**
  Dominique Wisler

Periodical Bibliography   **163**

For Further Discussion   **164**

Organizations to Contact   **167**

Bibliography of Books   **173**

Index   **177**

Why Consider Opposing Viewpoints?

> *"The only way in which a human being can make some approach to knowing the whole of a subject is by hearing what can be said about it by persons of every variety of opinion and studying all modes in which it can be looked at by every character of mind. No wise man ever acquired his wisdom in any mode but this."*
>
> *John Stuart Mill*

In our media-intensive culture it is not difficult to find differing opinions. Thousands of newspapers and magazines and dozens of radio and television talk shows resound with differing points of view. The difficulty lies in deciding which opinion to agree with and which "experts" seem the most credible. The more inundated we become with differing opinions and claims, the more essential it is to hone critical reading and thinking skills to evaluate these ideas. Opposing Viewpoints books address this problem directly by presenting stimulating debates that can be used to enhance and teach these skills. The varied opinions contained in each book examine many different aspects of a single issue. While examining these conveniently edited opposing views, readers can develop critical thinking skills such as the ability to compare and contrast authors' credibility, facts, argumentation styles, use of persuasive techniques, and other stylistic tools. In short, the Opposing Viewpoints Series is an ideal way to attain the higher-level thinking and reading skills so essential in a culture of diverse and contradictory opinions.

In addition to providing a tool for critical thinking, Opposing Viewpoints books challenge readers to question their own strongly held opinions and assumptions. Most people form their opinions on the basis of upbringing, peer pressure, and personal, cultural, or professional bias. By reading carefully balanced opposing views, readers must directly confront new ideas as well as the opinions of those with whom they disagree. This is not to simplistically argue that everyone who reads opposing views will—or should—change his or her opinion. Instead, the series enhances readers' understanding of their own views by encouraging confrontation with opposing ideas. Careful examination of others' views can lead to the readers' understanding of the logical inconsistencies in their own opinions, perspective on why they hold an opinion, and the consideration of the possibility that their opinion requires further evaluation.

Evaluating Other Opinions

To ensure that this type of examination occurs, Opposing Viewpoints books present all types of opinions. Prominent spokespeople on different sides of each issue as well as well-known professionals from many disciplines challenge the reader. An additional goal of the series is to provide a forum for other, less known, or even unpopular viewpoints. The opinion of an ordinary person who has had to make the decision to cut off life support from a terminally ill relative, for example, may be just as valuable and provide just as much insight as a medical ethicist's professional opinion. The editors have two additional purposes in including these less known views. One, the editors encourage readers to respect others' opinions—even when not enhanced by professional credibility. It is only by reading or listening to and objectively evaluating others' ideas that one can determine whether they are worthy of consideration. Two, the inclusion of such viewpoints encourages the important critical thinking skill of objectively evaluating an author's credentials and bias. This evaluation will illuminate an author's reasons for taking a particular stance on an issue and will aid in readers' evaluation of the author's ideas.

It is our hope that these books will give readers a deeper understanding of the issues debated and an appreciation of the complexity of even seemingly simple issues when good and honest people disagree. This awareness is particularly important in a democratic society such as ours in which people enter into public debate to determine the common good. Those with whom one disagrees should not be regarded as enemies but rather as people whose views deserve careful examination and may shed light on one's own.

Thomas Jefferson once said that "difference of opinion leads to inquiry, and inquiry to truth." Jefferson, a broadly educated man, argued that "if a nation expects to be ignorant and free . . . it expects what never was and never will be." As individuals and as a nation, it is imperative that we consider the opinions of others and examine them with skill and discernment. The Opposing Viewpoints Series is intended to help readers achieve this goal.

David L. Bender and Bruno Leone,
Founders

Introduction

> "It's my understanding that one of the officers spoke the word 'black' during the incident. Why would a person do that if race wasn't involved?"
>
> —Lt. Simon Hargrove,
> president of the Black Organization
> of Police, New Orleans, USA Today,
> April 5, 2006

In mid-October 2005, Robert Davis returned to New Orleans to check on several family homes damaged weeks earlier by Hurricane Katrina. The sixty-four-year-old retired schoolteacher was walking along Bourbon Street in the city's famous French Quarter at around 8:00 p.m. when he was beaten by two New Orleans police officers. Davis is black. The officers are white.

In the same incident, a camera crew from the Associated Press Television Network was roughed up by a third cop for filming the scene, and two other witnesses, volunteer relief workers visiting New Orleans to assist with hurricane cleanup, were forcibly detained in handcuffs, facedown on the sidewalk, because they told an officer they wanted to file a police report about what they had seen.

In December 2005, Anthony Hayes, a thirty-eight-year-old mentally ill New Orleans resident, was fatally shot with nine bullets from three different guns while surrounded by more than a dozen armed police officers. Hayes was wielding a knife, but was backing away from police, who followed him with guns drawn. When asked why the suspect hadn't simply been disabled by gunshots, considering how many police officers were present on the scene to contain him, Police Chief Warren Riley justified the officers' actions on the basis of training protocols, saying, "The vast majority of police departments—state, local and federal—are trained to shoot to kill . . . either in the head or the chest area."

In April 2006, Jonie Pratt, a New Orleans schoolteacher on furlough since Hurricane Katrina, was pulled over by police in front of her home in a middle-class neighborhood of the city. She was yanked from the car by her hair and beaten against the car several times before her arms were twisted behind her and handcuffed. She was sprayed in the face with Mace, shoved to the ground, and kicked in the head. She ended up with a broken wrist, a black eye, and other facial injuries.

What crime did Pratt commit to warrant such attention? She had apparently run a stop sign two blocks from home and then decided to drive to the supposed safety of her own neighborhood before pulling over in response to the flashing lights of the police car behind her. The police officers, who didn't believe her when she said she had stopped in front of her own house, are white. Pratt is black—and is married to Desmond Pratt, a ten-year veteran of the New Orleans police force. Her sister is a three-year member of the department, as well. Her mother-in-law, who was at the Pratt home babysitting for the couple's children at the time of the incident, reportedly shouted, "Stop that, that's Officer Pratt's wife!" Pratt was not released from the handcuffs, however, until several black officers arrived on the scene.

Given that all these incidents occurred within weeks or months after the devastation of Hurricane Katrina, an outside observer might conclude that the police officers involved were suffering from post-traumatic stress disorder. A recent report suggests that this is, in fact, a mental health problem among the city's emergency workers, but the truth is, the New Orleans Police Department (NOPD) has had a long and infamous history of headline-grabbing police misconduct. In 1999, the organization Human Rights Watch identified the NOPD as the worst in the United States in terms of brutality and corruption.

During the 1990s, NOPD officers were arrested for a wide range of crimes, including bank robbery, shoplifting, drug dealing, rape, and murder. A report published in September 2000 by the Progressive Policy Institute noted that a 1994 corruption investigation led to the dismissal of two hundred NOPD officers. More than two dozen had been involved in protecting a cocaine supply network. Others had accepted tens of thousands of dollars in bribes. Before the investigation was complete, a witness was murdered, on orders from one of the police officers involved.

In 2002, a Police-Civilian Review Task Force recommended that the city hire an independent monitor to review what happens when civilians file complaints alleging NOPD brutality or wrongdoing. The task force itself had been created following the fatal shooting of an unarmed teenager two years earlier. After a city council hearing in 2003, however, no monitor was hired. Throughout 2004, NOPD officers were arrested for crimes including conspiracy to rob a bank, theft, shoplifting, aggravated kidnapping, and extortion. In one of these cases, a sixteen-year veteran of the force threatened to arrest a woman if she wouldn't have sex with him. Then, in August 2005, barely a week before Hurricane Katrina hit, a two-year veteran officer was charged with aggravated rape and kidnapping after being accused of stopping a bicyclist, driving her to a remote location, and sexually assaulting her.

Following in the wake of Hurricane Katrina in the Gulf Coast region, national news media reports surfaced alleging NOPD misconduct, including assault, looting of homes and businesses, and neglect of duty. Conditioned by images of selflessness and sacrifice exhibited by rescue and emergency workers in New York City during the chaos of September 11, 2001, and the days following that tragedy, many viewers were inclined to think generously of the NOPD, assuming that most reports of alleged misconduct were based on erroneous information or a misinterpretation of what actually happened.

However, displaced New Orleanians, particularly those who once lived in the poor, black neighborhoods of the city, were not fooled. In their experience, racial profiling, use of unnecessary force, planting of evidence, public strip searches, and verbal abuse and threats are to be expected from their city's police officers.

Ironically, even as national media interest in New Orleans' post-Katrina recovery continued during the months following the hurricane, relatively little attention was paid to the stories of people like Robert Davis, Anthony Hayes, and Jonie Pratt. Is police brutality now so commonplace that even videotaped incidents don't merit much air time? *Police Brutality: Opposing Viewpoints* examines a wide range of issues related to police misconduct and brutality in the following chapters: Is Misconduct in Law Enforcement a Serious Problem? What Factors Cause Police Brutality? Does the War on Terror Invite Law-Enforcement Abuse? How Can Police Misconduct Be Reduced? The viewpoints presented in this volume debate the effectiveness, legality, and ethical merits of the practices that constitute contemporary police work.

CHAPTER 1

Is Misconduct in Law Enforcement a Serious Problem?

Chapter Preface

In April 1963, black civil rights leaders in Birmingham, Alabama, organized nonviolent protests and boycotts to bring an end to the segregation of the city's restaurants, public restrooms, and drinking fountains. Police Commissioner Eugene "Bull" Connor threatened to arrest anyone who joined the effort and amassed police officers to intimidate would-be protesters. Instead of putting an end to the action, however, the threats inspired more participation. Soon, hundreds of black men, women, and children of all ages began gathering daily to march in the streets, peacefully defying the all-white leadership of the city.

At first, the police engaged in mass arrests, sending black residents to jail for nothing more criminal than walking along a public street. When this proved to be ineffective as a deterrent, the police attacked the crowds with batons, police dogs, and high-pressure water hoses from the city's fire trucks, all with the blessing of the police commissioner. This officially sanctioned use of excessive force horrified television viewers and readers of newspapers worldwide. Images of white Birmingham police officers attacking seven- and eight-year-old black children with dogs and fire hoses were particularly offensive, even to many white southerners who supported segregation. Yet in 1963, there was little expectation that these—or any other—police officers would be held accountable for having committed acts of violence against unarmed victims.

Fast-forward nearly thirty years to March 3, 1991, when a bystander with a handheld camcorder videotaped a police confrontation between four white police officers and Rodney King, a black Los Angeles resident. The riveting—and non-stop—television coverage that followed once again forced Americans to confront images of what appeared to be racially motivated police brutality. This time, however, public expectations were different. Even taking into account the possibility that King may have committed some criminal activity before the videotape began rolling, many Americans were offended by the display of brutal physical force used by four uniformed white men against a lone black man, particularly when the blows and kicks continued after King appeared to be subdued. And whether or not they believed the officers were justified in their use of force, most viewers assumed that the police officers involved in this incident would have to defend themselves against charges that they had crossed the line into excessive force.

Video imagery is a powerful force in shaping public perception, but events captured on tape are subject to interpretation. Ironically, the same videotape that led to indictments against the officers in the Rodney King case was used to successfully defend them in their first trial; however, the existence of a real-time video record of the event activates a certain "seeing is believing" factor in viewers. As Alan Tieger, a prosecuting attorney in the 1993 federal trial of the four officers indicted in the beating of Rodney King, said, "The common wisdom about videos and about video evidence is that it's the infallible witness—a witness whose memory doesn't fade, whose perceptions don't influence the way in which the event is recorded."

More than a decade after a televised bit of amateur video elevated the issue of police brutality to national debate, Americans still don't agree on what they "see" in images of police use of force. Is it justified? Or is it brutality? The question of whether law enforcement misconduct is a serious problem is debated in the following chapter.

> "*Despite major improvements in police practices [since 1981] reports of alleged police misconduct and abuse continue to spread through the nation.*"

Police Brutality Is Widespread

U.S. Commission on Civil Rights

In the following viewpoint, the U.S. Commission on Civil Rights asserts that police brutality is prevalent in the United States. Incidents of shocking brutality occur on a regular basis, the authors contend. The commission calls for improved officer training and discipline as well as departmental reforms to reduce misconduct. The U.S. Commission on Civil Rights was formed in 1957 as a fact-finding group charged with making recommendations to the government.

As you read, consider the following questions:

1. Does the U.S. Civil Rights Commission believe police misconduct has disappeared, stayed the same, or gained more of a spotlight since the original *Guardians* report was published in 1981?

2. According to the commission, what "agonizing" reality exists alongside crime-reduction statistics?

U.S. Commission on Civil Rights, "Who Is Guarding the Guardians?: A Report on Police Policies and Civil Rights in America," http://www.usccr.gov/pubs/guard/main.htm, 2000. Reproduced by permission.

3. According to the commission, racial profiling compromises what two types of principles?

The report by the U.S. Commission on Civil Rights titled *Who Is Guarding the Guardians?* [published in October 1981] remains a major publication on police practices and civil rights. . . .

Despite major improvements in police practices [since 1981] reports of alleged police misconduct and abuse continue to spread through the nation. As a major policy issue, police misconduct has not disappeared, but rather gained more of a spotlight since *Guardians* with the advent of issues such as racial profiling. The following stories represent a fraction of the incidents that have led up to the publication of this report.

Shocking Incidents

The mere mention of the name "Rodney King" conjures the shocking images captured by an amateur video of an African American man surrounded and beaten by Los Angeles police officers.

In 1997, the beating and assault of Abner Louima while in custody in a New York City precinct stunned the country.

In 1998, two New Jersey state troopers opened fire into a van with three African American and one Hispanic male passengers on the New Jersey Turnpike. The van was allegedly speeding at a rate of 19 miles per hour above the 55-miles-per-hour speed limit. The troopers claimed that the 11 shots fired into the van were in self-defense.

Four other New Jersey state troopers escaped federal prosecution for opening fire into a car in 1999 after the driver failed to stop for an alleged traffic violation. The driver allegedly led the police on a 15-mile chase. The evidence was insufficient to sustain federal criminal civil rights claims.

More Scandals

Later, Amadou Diallo, an unarmed West African immigrant, died in the vestibule of his home when four New York City police officers fired 41 shots at him. The officers involved in the fatal shooting of Mr. Diallo were acquitted of all charges.

The Los Angeles Police Department, already battered with numerous allegations of misconduct, found itself involved in another scandal—this time involving its Rampart Division. Officers were charged with planting evidence on suspects and "covering it up." The scandal reinforced the public's perception that corruption still plagues the police department.

The New York City Police Department faced allegations in June 2000 that its officers did not respond to the cries for help from women in Central Park who were being sexually assaulted at a public event.

In July 2000, a New York City grand jury cleared an undercover narcotics officer in the March shooting of an unarmed security guard. The guard, Patrick Dorismond, became upset when an undercover police officer approached him to buy drugs.

In Philadelphia, Thomas Jones was allegedly beaten by a group of police officers that caught him after two car chases, one involving Jones' driving a police vehicle.

On the same day as the Philadelphia incident, police officers in Lawrenceville, Georgia, were videotaped beating Marshall Dwight Studdard. Mr. Studdard allegedly led police on a three-county chase when police finally caught up with him.

Former Los Alamos National Laboratory scientist Wen Ho Lee was charged with "59 counts of violating nuclear security" and held in solitary pretrial federal confinement for nine months. The one-time heated prosecution of Lee "virtually collapsed . . . when an FBI agent recanted testimony in which he said Lee lied about his purpose for downloading the nuclear information."

Steve Kelley. © 1991 Steve Kelley, *The San Diego Union-Tribune*. Reprinted with permission of Steve Kelley. *Times-Picayune*, New Orleans.

Prince Jones, a Howard University student, died from a fatal gunshot wound inflicted by a Prince George's County (Maryland) police officer who followed him in an unmarked sport utility vehicle because "a vehicle matching the description of the car driven by Prince Jones was linked to a weapon stolen from a Prince George's County police vehicle." Prince Jones was shot "five times in the torso and once in the forearm, all from behind."

Agonizing Reality

As a result of the incidents described above, the terms "racial profiling" and "community policing" have entered the everyday vocabulary of many Americans. . . .

Law enforcement agencies have made great in-roads in reducing crime and the use of deadly force, but such progress comes at a cost. An agonizing reality exists alongside statistics showing a decrease in the use of deadly force by police officers and a reduction of crime in many communities: the persistence of police misconduct. For example, the fact that 11 people were shot down by police officers in New York City in 1999 compared with 41 in 1990 does not remove the specter of impending doom that visits ordinary law-abiding people of color during street encounters with police officers in the city. The errant behavior of a few abusive police officers, even in the absence of police shootings, can often destroy cooperative and strategic alliances between police departments and the communities they serve. When some citizens perceive and experience the police being unfair, inequitable, harsh, and/or arbitrary, and moreover, when these citizens come from groups that have historically experienced unfair and inappropriate police behavior, such perceptions and experiences deride the very concept of fair and equitable treatment under the law and erode the bonds of civil society.

This is not to say that the laudatory reduction in fatal shootings by police officers is unimportant. The recorded decreases in police shootings exhibit a meaningful illustration of the progress that law enforcement departments can achieve when reform efforts are targeted and emphasized in training and professional discipline for the use of deadly force. It is significant, however, that cultural training practices and uniformly employed discipline are lacking in other important areas of police work. Additional police reforms are required to reduce civil rights violations where they continue to occur in the course of complex police investigations and in response to questionable crime reduction strategies.

A Complex Problem

For example, a compelling case can be made for providing better training and harsher discipline to law enforcement officials to prevent officers from transgressing constitutional requirements for initiating a legal stop based on individualized

Brutality Is Part of Society's Fabric

It's going to take revolution to end police brutality once and for all because police brutality is built into the very fabric of this society. We live in a society divided into haves and have nots. The haves, the capitalist class, rule over the majority of the people and use force to suppress the people here in this country and around the world that they rip off. Enforcing the unjust conditions that their system forces millions in the U.S. to endure requires a police force capable of inflicting unspeakable brutality and murder. Not every cop has murdered someone, but most have helped cover up these abuses or looked the other way when they go down.

Revolutionary Worker, *October 29, 2000. www.rwor.org.*

suspicion. Currently, an urgent need exists to halt the frequent police practice of disproportionately stopping individuals of color based on statistical probabilities and demographics. Racial profiling compromises civil rights and constitutional principles. Such incidents often leave blameless, upstanding persons with emotional scars, if not physical injuries. These scars and injuries cause these individuals to remain apprehensive about the prospect of future adverse encounters with police officers. Left with no assurances that effective disciplinary actions will be taken or reforms implemented, the injured individuals maintain lingering doubts about the objectivity of persons who wear badges, carry guns, and make critical judgments about who is and who is not a criminal suspect.

As the Cato Institute determined in a report about New York City's Street Crime Unit that was released in 2000, "experience has shown that stop-and-frisk tactics unnecessarily endanger the police, the suspect and bystanders. Policymakers in

New York and elsewhere should discontinue the freewheeling stop-and-frisk searches and restore the constitutional standard of probable cause without delay."

The Commission recognizes and reiterates that the adverse actions of some officers are not representative of all law enforcement professionals. Law-abiding officers should not have to pay for the crimes committed by a few whose actions are memorialized in news headlines. The problem of police misconduct, however, is too pervasive and complex to be reduced to simply blaming a few rogue law enforcement officers. It is important to note that the problem of police misconduct is not limited to white officers but may include officers of color. Indeed, police practices and policies as a whole, which include training, use of deadly force, oversight, and the police culture, contribute to the problem. Correcting these issues and addressing community concerns are the only legitimate means of ensuring the protection of the civil rights of all Americans.

> *"Although the cases of police shootings mentioned in recent headlines are dreadful, there is no empirical evidence that police brutality is rampant in the nation."*

The Extent of Police Brutality Is Exaggerated

Russell G. Redenbaugh

Russell G. Redenbaugh served on the U.S. Commission on Civil Rights from 1990 to 2005. He was affiliated with no political party. In the following viewpoint he disagrees with key points presented by his fellow commissioners in Revisiting "Who Is Guarding the Guardians?", *a 2000 report on police practices. The report was highly critical of the police, arguing that misconduct is rampant. According to Redenbaugh, the report minimizes the improvements that have been made in police conduct and exaggerates the extent of police brutality.*

As you read, consider the following questions:

1. According to Redenbaugh, what "meaningful change" has happened in cities like New York, demonstrating progress in police reform?

Russell G. Redenbaugh, "Dissenting Statement of Commissioner Russell G. Redenbaugh," http://www.usccr.gov/pubs/guard/stat.htm, 2000. Reproduced by permission.

2. What are two factors that affect a police officer's decision to use force, according to Redenbaugh?

3. What are two examples of training classes that the New York Police Department has used to help officers deal with real-life situations without force, as cited by the author?

The report [*Revisiting "Who Is Guarding the Guardians?"*] fails to give a clear picture of police reforms over the last two decades. On the one hand, it concludes that there has been "very little meaningful change" since the initial release of *Who Is Guarding the Guardians?* At the same time, the Chairperson of the Commission has also admitted, in ... press statements, that there has been "a lot of progress" since the 1981 report.

Certainly, there are many signs of meaningful changes. In major cities like New York, for example, significant reductions in violent crime have been accompanied by a dramatic decline in police use of force. Additional meaningful changes have resulted from the proliferation of community policing programs and civilian review panels, the development of training strategies to improve law enforcement response and to reduce risk and liability, and the implementation of computer technology to enhance early warning capabilities. But the present report tends to downplay these signs of progress, concluding that better policing often has come "at a terrible price" for minority communities, "which seem to bear the brunt" of police misconduct. With this kind of sweeping indictment, the report demonstrates that it is not really interested in the data it purports to gather....

Police Use of Force

In order to protect citizens, police officers are entrusted with the enormous responsibility of having the authority to use force, including deadly force, under certain circumstances. De-

Chuck Asay. Reproduced by permission.

cisions on use of force are affected by several factors, including the degree of threatening behavior displayed by the suspect, state laws, police department policy, and training. What we do know, from experts and police officers alike, is that the media portrayal of police brutality is often significantly different from reality. Although the cases of police shootings mentioned in recent headlines are dreadful, there is no empirical evidence that police brutality is rampant in the nation, as suggested by this report.

The report also errs in choosing to look at these problems mainly through the prism of race. For example, on the basis of anecdotes and "perceptions," the report reaches the conclusion "that law enforcement officers disproportionately target [minority] communities because of misperceptions based on their racial and ethnic backgrounds, rather than crime patterns or citizen complaints." The report implies that police shootings are primarily a racial problem, one that could be resolved by "diversity" or "cultural training" initiatives.

Police Reflect a Violent Society

Since no one has mentioned it, allow me say it: Police are not the problem.

Officers are not the racist, trigger-happy, brutal, heavy-handed monsters as portrayed in the media. Officers reflect the society they are a part of.

All of us are the problem, because we have consistently failed to address the underlying social issues that have turned us into the most violent and the most unequal society in the industrialized nations.

Sunil Dutta, L.A. Daily News, March 6, 2005. www.dailynews.com.

This appears to be an over-simplification of the issue. It is instructive to look at recent studies which indicate that incidents of police use of force (meaning both lawful and unlawful actions where an officer employs physical coercion) tend to be intraracial, meaning that the officers and citizens involved are more likely to be of the same race and ethnicity. In 1997, the fatal shooting of suspected black felons by black officers was almost four times higher than the fatal shooting rate of suspected black felons by white officers. The black police officer shooting rate of suspected black felons was 5.47 per 10,000 black officers, while the fatal shooting rate of suspected black felons by white officers was 1.41 per 10,000 white officers.

Flawed Prescriptions for Reform

In its tendency to point to selected, high-profile cases as examples of "incessant" police misconduct and endemic police racism, the report stresses "the importance of diversity" and the need to make law enforcement agencies more "culturally competent." In [an Autumn 2000] article on "How to Train Cops," published by the Manhattan Institute, Heather Mac

Donald explains the dangers of the "cultural sensitivity" approach. From direct observation of a "cultural competence" course at New York's Police Academy, Ms. Mac Donald contends that these sessions are "wildly irrelevant to the real problems of policing." Mandating such courses also represents "a huge opportunity cost" in terms of time that could be spent on instruction—particularly, communication skills—to improve police response to the situations confronting them every day, sometimes fatally. As Ms. Mac Donald concludes: "Reality, not racism, is the biggest challenge for the police."

By emphasizing culture over competence, the report misses the opportunity to provide any in-depth discussion of police training methods that have proven effective in enhancing the ability of police to deal with real-life situations without having to resort to the use of force. The NYPD's [New York Police Department's] "In-Service Tactical Training" and its "verbal judo" courses are just two examples of this kind of training. Effective and professional policing, not an irrelevant "cultural competence" curriculum, is the key to achieving the dual goals of crime reduction and protection of citizens' civil rights.

External vs. Internal Controls

Another major problem is the report's conclusion that since the "guardians" are unable to "guard" themselves (because of a "police culture" inclined to protect wrongdoers within the ranks), what is needed is wider use of "external controls." In order to "police the police," the report proposes a number of heavy-handed recommendations for federal monitors, special prosecutors, and civilian review boards with final say over local investigations of police misconduct incidents.

This kind of adversarial approach runs counter to testimony the Commission received at [a June 2000] briefing from Hubert Williams, president of the Police Foundation. As Mr. Williams affirmed in his written statement: "While both internal and external accountability of the police are required, internal accountability is more effective at deterring police misconduct." Mr. Williams went on to emphasize the need for innovative technologies such as the Risk Analysis Management System and the Quality of Service Indicator, which strengthen internal accountability through the collection and analysis of key performance-related data.

Prejudice has no place in the enforcement of the laws of this nation. Police misconduct and racial profiling are morally reprehensible and an ineffective way to enforce the law.

While there is no question that police misconduct does occur, there is no evidence that points to an epidemic of such misconduct.

| "A rash of antiterrorism laws and policies ... have resulted in unlawful police practices that place enormous constraints on free-speech guarantees."

Antiterrorism Policies Result in Police Abuse of Dissenters

Heidi Boghosian

In the following viewpoint Heidi Boghosian presents evidence that the U.S. Department of Justice knowingly allows the police to hinder rights of free speech and assembly. During protests of the Bush administration's security policies following the September 11, 2001, terrorist attacks, for example, police used excessive force to intimidate the mostly peaceful activists, she claims. Moreover, the author charges the department with failing to prosecute law enforcers who engage in unlawful practices regarding civil rights. Boghosian is executive director of the National Lawyers Guild.

As you read, consider the following questions:

1. According to Boghosian, how does the U.S. government routinely depict those who speak out against U.S. government policies?

Heidi Boghosian, *The Assault on Free Speech, Public Assembly, and Dissent: A National Lawyer's Guild Report on Government Violations of First Amendment Rights in the United States*. Great Barrington, MA: North River Press, 2004. Reproduced by permission.

2. What did the Ninth Court rule was the government's proper response to First-Amendment-protected activities that had resulted in violence in the past, according to the author?

3. When John Ashcroft spoke to a police group in Phoenix in 2001, what was his attitude toward the use of the law to prosecute police departments, according to Boghosian?

This [viewpoint] documents the ongoing reaction of law enforcement to the legal exercise of free speech in the United States. It finds that legitimate concerns regarding public safety have been abused by the United States Department of Justice. The abuses have been so aggressive that rights of free assembly and free speech guaranteed by the First Amendment of the United States Constitution are simply no longer available to the citizens of this country.

This [viewpoint] surveys federal and local police actions in the United States during the period 1999–2004 involving lawful public expressions of dissent and free speech. All of the police activities cited are from firsthand experience of the National Lawyers Guild, the oldest human rights organization in the country. Hundreds of Guild attorneys, legal workers, and law students around the country have served both as legal observers at First Amendment protected public assemblies and as counsel to individuals who sought to air their views at such public assemblies.

First Amendment Rights

The conclusion of this [viewpoint] is that rather than protecting First Amendment rights of United States citizens and prosecuting police abuses as it ought to do, the Justice Department under Attorney General John Ashcroft has systematically encouraged these abuses and acted as a cheerleader for government officials using excessive force and abusing their authority against citizens engaged in free speech. By making enemies of those who speak out, law-enforcement agencies engage in unnecessary, costly, and dangerous practices against law-abiding individuals, wasting limited resources and frightening many from voicing their opinions. And by turning a blind eye to rampant and systemic police unlawfulness, the Attorney General is abrogating his duty to uphold the laws of the United States.

In times of crisis, governmental respect diminishes for the protections of speech embodied in the First and Fourteenth Amendments to the Constitution of the United States. Alexander Meiklejohn [an American educator and civil libertarian who lived 1872–1964] warned that interpreting the First Amendment in a fashion that authorizes the legislature to balance security against freedom of speech denies the essential purpose and meaning of the amendment. The security of a nation pledged to self-governance, he wrote, is never endangered by its people. Yet over the past few years a rash of antiterrorism laws and policies—both official and unofficial— have resulted in unlawful police practices that place enormous constraints on free-speech guarantees. The [George W. Bush] administration has supported these practices, justifying them as necessary during a period of national crisis.

Most of these practices have not, in fact, made this country safer and are often used as pretextual justification to broadcast the message that the act of engaging in First Amendment protected activity is unlawful. The government routinely depicts as public enemies, and even potential terrorists, those who speak out against U.S. government policies. In contrast to the administration, however, most Americans favor the freedom to voice unpopular opinions: In a 2003 survey by the First Amendment Center to measure public support for First Amendment freedoms, 95% of respondents agreed that individuals should be allowed to express unpopular opinions in this country, and two-thirds supported the right of any group to hold a rally for a cause, even if that cause is offensive to others.

Major Trends

Several major trends have given rise to a host of police practices that not only unlawfully interfere with the exercise of protected speech but also result in affirmative harm to innocent individuals. The trends are:

- **Punishment absent unlawful activity**, violating the Fourth and Fifth Amendments and giving rise to state claims of assault and battery, false imprisonment, trespass on the person, negligence in causing injuries, and negligent hiring, screening, retention, supervision, and training of officers, as well as conspiracy and malicious prosecution.

- **Police-initiated violence**, a dynamic acknowledged by the United Nations Commission on Human Rights, the District of Columbia Report on the Investigation of the Metropolitan Police Department's Policy and Practice in Handling Demonstrations in the District of Columbia, and the Independent Review Panel that investigated the actions of the Miami-Dade Police Department and the Miami-Dade Corrections and Rehabilitation Department during the 2003 FTAA [Free Trade Area of the Americas] ministerial.

- **Failure of the Department of Justice (DOJ), under the leadership of Attorney General Ashcroft, to prosecute police officers and police departments** for engaging in unlawful practices that violate the civil rights of individuals around the country.

These trends and practices are informed in part by the DOJ's enactment of domestic terrorism laws following the attacks of September 11, 2001, and the recent relaxation of the

Toles. © 2005 distributed by Universal Press Syndicate.

1976 Attorney General guidelines on FBI [Federal Bureau of Investigation] surveillance, allowing spying on and infiltration of political groups and meetings. With the hasty passage of the USA PATRIOT Act in 2001, those who criticize the government or maintain ties with international political movements may find themselves under investigation for domestic terrorism. The term "terrorism" is defined so broadly in the act that anyone who engages in traditional forms of protest may arguably fall under its description.

Punishment Absent Unlawful Activity

Although greatly exacerbated following the 2001 attacks, an increase had been evident for several preceding years in massive police presence and punishment absent unlawful activity at large demonstrations. Such punishment of those wishing to exercise their First Amendment rights has taken several forms, including content-based permitting, arrests in anticipation of actions, the setting of record-high bails of up to $1 million for misdemeanors, and the use of chemical weapons and "less lethal" rounds against crowds without provocation. Activities that cause individuals to fear engaging in speech because of possible punishment are profoundly dangerous to the proper functioning of any democracy. In addition, the government generates erroneous and negative portrayals of protesters that are repeated uncritically by the media and that perpetuate frightening stereotypes. Furthermore, anticipatory punishment is illegal: In *Collins v. Jordan*, the Ninth Circuit reaffirmed that First Amendment activity may not be banned merely because similar activity resulted in instances of violence in the past: "The courts have held that the proper response to potential and actual violence is for the government to ensure an adequate police presence and to arrest those who actually engage in such conduct rather than to suppress legitimate First Amendment conduct as a prophylactic measure."

It should be noted that police violence has escalated since the 1999 World Trade Organization meeting, when thousands of individuals of all ages and backgrounds flocked to Seattle for protests. According to the final report of the Seattle City Council's World Trade Organization Accountability Review Committee, what police described as massive violence by protesters was in fact an abdication of police and city leaders' responsibility during the planning process. The report concluded that Seattle police chief Norman Stamper's "failure to provide leadership . . . contributed to the lack of proper planning, which placed the lives of police officers and citizens at risk and contributed to the violation of protesters' constitutional rights."

The suppression of legitimate First Amendment activities by legions of police and government agents suited in body armor and engaging in paramilitary tactics has a terrifying effect on demonstrators and creates an atmosphere of violence. Such tactics frighten protesters and encourage aggressive behavior among police officers, resulting in unnecessary confrontation and injuries.

FBI Encouraged Police Spying

On May 30, 2002, Attorney General Ashcroft amended the Attorney General's guidelines on FBI domestic spying. Under the new guidelines, agents may use data-mining services and may search . . . public databases and the Internet for leads to terrorist activities; both of those activities were formerly forbidden. The revised guidelines also shift the authority to begin counterterrorism inquiries from FBI headquarters to special agents in charge of FBI field offices. Nearly thirty years earlier, in 1976, Attorney General Edward Levi wrote guidelines limiting federal investigative power that became known as the Levi guidelines. That revision came about following the shocking revelations of the 1975–76 hearings of a Senate committee, the Church Commission, which exposed the surveillance, infiltration, and disruption tactics used against U.S. political groups by the FBI and the CIA [Central Intelligence Agency] in the COINTELPRO program. Central to the new guidelines was that investigations could only be initiated if "specific and articulable facts" indicated criminal activity. In 1983, Attorney General William French Smith relaxed the Levi guidelines so that a full investigation could be opened if there existed a "reasonable indication" of criminal activity.

After the Attorney General's guidelines were loosened by Ashcroft, the FBI, in an internal newsletter in 2003, encouraged agents to step up interviews with antiwar activists "for plenty of reasons, chief of which it will enhance the paranoia endemic in such circles and will further serve to get the point across that there is an FBI agent behind every mailbox." This language reveals an "us vs. them" approach that vilifies the subject of surveillance. On November 23, 2003, news broke of

Miami Paramilitaries

[After Miami Chief of Police John Timoney's handling of protesters at the 2003 meeting of the Free Trade Area of the Americas (FTAA)], no one should call what Timoney runs in Miami a police force. It's a paramilitary group. Thousands of soldiers, dressed in khaki uniforms with full black body armor and gas masks, marching in unison through the streets, banging batons against their shields, chanting, "back . . . back . . . back." There were armored personnel carriers and helicopters.

The forces fired indiscriminately into crowds of unarmed protesters. Scores of people were hit with skin-piercing rubber bullets; thousands were gassed with an array of chemicals. On several occasions, police fired loud concussion grenades into the crowds. Police shocked people with electric tazers. Demonstrators were shot in the back as they retreated. One young guy's apparent crime was holding his fingers in a peace sign in front of the troops. They shot him multiple times, including once in the stomach at point blank range.

Jeremy Scahill, "The Miami Model:
Paramilitaries, Embedded Journalists, and Illegal Protests,"
November 24, 2003. http://ftaaime.org.

a classified FBI memorandum dated October 15, 2003, sent to more than 15,000 local law-enforcement organizations days before antiwar demonstrations were held in Washington and San Francisco, encouraging police to report potentially unlawful activities of protesters to the FBI Joint Terrorism Task Force. Examples of "criminal" activity cited were using tape recorders and video cameras and wearing sunglasses or scarves as protection from pepper spray. The memo revealed that the FBI had collected detailed information on the tactics, training, and organization of antiwar demonstrators. The memorandum contained information on how some demonstrators prepared for protests and used the Internet to raise funds for legal defense.

Relaxed Restrictions

The relaxing of restrictions on governmental domestic spying and the FBI memorandum suggest the existence of an ongoing, national drive to collect intelligence related to protests through local law enforcement. There is compelling evidence of the existence of this ongoing effort: Civil libertarians have sued the government to find out why their names are on a "no fly" list intended to stop suspected terrorists from boarding planes; federal and local authorities in Denver [Colorado] and Fresno [California] have spied on antiwar demonstrators and infiltrated planning meetings; and the New York Police Department questioned many arrestees at demonstrations about their political affiliations and their opinions on the war in Iraq. In addition, the government issued subpoenas for the records of the National Lawyers Guild's Drake University chapter and to compel antiwar activists to appear before a grand jury months after they attended a Guild-sponsored antiwar conference on the university's campus in 2003.

An overarching consequence of the government's accelerated suppression of free expression and its failure to prosecute police departments for aggressive and unlawful conduct is that individuals are intimidated from voicing their views. Would-be protesters or communities frequently targeted by the police, many of whom are thinking about exercising their First Amendment rights publicly for the first time, may decide that it is not worth the risk of encountering police violence and possible arrest. This is particularly true in the case of individuals who have police records or who have concerns about their immigration status. . . .

Police Abuse

After passage of the Crime Control and Law Enforcement Act of 1994, the Department of Justice was tasked with collecting data on the frequency and types of abuse complaints filed nationwide. The 1994 Act included a new statute under which the DOJ may sue for declaratory relief (a statement of the governing law) and equitable relief (an order to abide by the law with specific instructions describing actions that must be taken) if any governmental authority or person acting on behalf of any governmental authority engages in "a pattern or practice of conduct by law enforcement officers ... that deprives persons of rights, privileges, or immunities secured or protected by the Constitution or laws of the United States."

In 1996 the DOJ initiated several federal pattern-and-practice civil investigations of police departments, and subsequently it forged agreements with police departments around the country. The DOJ's Civil Rights Division investigated police misconduct in Steubenvile, Ohio and Pittsburgh and worked out agreements with those cities to institute reforms aimed at curbing practices that constituted violations rather than risk the DOJ's taking a case to court for injunctive action. DOJ-proposed reforms included improving policies and training on the use of force, instituting more effective reporting mechanisms and disciplinary procedures, and establishing early-warning systems to identify officers engaging in abuse or at risk of doing so. In June 2001, the Los Angeles Police Department and the City of Los Angeles entered into a consent decree requiring change in such areas as complaint investigations and documentation of the use of force. A consent decree is an agreement between involved parties submitted in writing to a judge. Once approved by the judge it becomes legally binding.

Changes Under Ashcroft

When Attorney General Ashcroft took office, however, there were significant changes in the DOJ's approach to oversight of police misconduct. The Attorney General has shown an aversion to entering into consent decrees, rather preferring to enter into memoranda of understanding with police departments, and often lifting existing consent decrees.

For example, in 1997 the DOJ intervened in a civil-rights lawsuit against police in Pittsburgh and helped design systemic reforms. Under John Ashcroft's authority, however, the DOJ's Civil Rights Division joined with Pittsburgh officials in 2002 in asking a federal judge to lift the consent decree, even though the court-appointed auditor had just documented several remaining problems. The court granted the Justice Department's motion in part, over the objection of the NAACP [National Association for the Advancement of Colored People], the ACLU [American Civil Liberties Union], and other groups that had initiated the lawsuit prior to the DOJ's involvement.

In another example of Attorney General Ashcroft's shying away from consent decrees, the DOJ requested an order partially lifting the consent decree between the State of New Jersey and the Department of Justice entered into in 1999 amid allegations that police were engaging in racial profiling. A U.S. District Judge signed an order in early April 2004 ending federal oversight of the Office of Professional Standards, the internal affairs unit of the New Jersey police. Civil-rights leaders were critical of the judge's decision, saying that the consent decree should not be lifted in pieces.

Good Will

Mr. Ashcroft publicly indicated his reluctance to use the law to prosecute police departments in his remarks to the Fraternal Order of Police in its 55th Biennial National Conference in Phoenix on August 14, 2001. In explaining how in 1999 the District of Columbia Metropolitan Police Department [MPD] "asked for help to determine if its officers used excessive force in dealing with members of the public," he described how the Justice Department began to "fix the problem:"

> No court orders were involved. No consent decrees were issued. Through hard work and good will on both sides we were able to produce results.

Consent decrees are generally regarded as critical in implementing institutional reform in police departments. Former U.S. Assistant Attorney General John Dunne has noted that consent decrees force top-level police officials to commit to reform. He also supports bringing pattern-and-practice suits and says they cast "a whole new light on the matter of Civil Rights Division responsibility." Indeed, Mr. Ashcroft's "hard work and good will" approach clearly had no long-term effect on the MPD's pattern and practice of using excessive force against members of the public, as a 2004 report by the D.C. City Council's Committee on the Judiciary explains in detail.

By not exercising federal prosecutorial oversight of national, systemic police violations of civil rights, Attorney General Ashcroft is essentially acting as a conspirator with police departments around the nation to deprive people of their constitutionally protected rights.

| "Our increasingly federalized police seem all too willing in these days of the War on Terror to employ terror tactics whenever they can get away with it."

The War on Terror Has Led to More Use of Excessive Force

Llewellyn H. Rockwell Jr.

In the following viewpoint Llewellyn H. Rockwell Jr. explores a 2003 incident in which an unarmed African American man died after a struggle with Cincinnati police. According to Rockwell, the police used excessive force, a practice Rockwell believes has become more prevalent since the September 11, 2001, terrorist attacks. He believes that law-enforcement officers view the War on Terror as license to use brutal police methods. Rockwell is a writer who describes himself as "an opponent of the central state, its wars, and its socialism." He is an officer of the Center for Libertarian Studies and the Mises Institute, the latter devoted to the thought of Ludwig von Mises (1881–1973), an Austrian economist and social philosopher.

As you read, consider the following questions:

1. How many times did police hit Nathaniel Jones with a metal baton, according to Rockwell?

Llewellyn H. Rockwell Jr., "That Cincinnati Beating," lewrockwell.com, December 4, 2003. Reproduced by permission.

2. According to the author, good sense suggests two better ways police could have dealt with Jones instead of beating him. What are they?

3. What condition do the "armed agents of the state" seem to be experiencing, according to Rockwell?

Ludwig von Mises often reminded his readers that the state is all about beating, hanging, and killing; that when you advocate a law or a regulation, you are effectively granting the state the permission to kill non-compliers. This, and not compassion, is the essence of statecraft. And while plenty of foreigners know all about the killing power of the American state, few in the US pay much attention, unless it involves race.

Thus has the [2003] Cincinnati case of a police killing gained attention, especially the snippet that shows the police pounding a black man to his death. Like the Rodney King case in Los Angeles, this one seems destined to inflame passions. Those who regard blacks as official victims, entitled to unending benefits at the expense of everyone else, revel in such scenes, if only because they make the redistributionist political agenda easier to enact and harder to object to. And those who want to centralize law enforcement like it too, because it seems to suggest that local police are abusive and in need of top-down control by the squeaky-clean saviors from on high.

Is Killing Ever Justified?

Using these scenes for political propaganda is effective because no person with an attachment to the idea of liberty is thrilled to see police beating anyone. The scene seems to embody a radical disparity in power, one person confronting a group of uniformed government agents who can legally kill anyone who struggles to be free of them. A police beating seems to sum up everything that is inherently wrong with the existing relationship between the individual and the state.

The Police Are Not Our Protectors

In the wake of September 11, [2001,] the police have become "heroes" and "saviors" who are above questioning and criticism. History is being rewritten—no longer is racial profiling considered a repulsive practice, but an accepted police procedure. In a recent court decision, New Jersey state troopers were cleared of any criminal responsibility for shooting and maiming four Black and Latino youth in an infamous case of racial profiling.

Revolutionary Worker, *March 10, 2002. www.rwor.org.*

That is not to say that beating and killing is never justified. A property owner can kill an intruder. A person defending his life against an attacker can kill. Killing can be justified as self-defense and even as punishment. These are established principles in law and morality.

The tough part is making the transition to the state and its relationship to individuals. Can the police legally kill someone simply because he resists arrest? Why are the police permitted to break the laws they allegedly enforce? They are permitted to speed, trespass, and rob in the name of cracking down on speeding, trespassing, and robbing. There is something about the institutionalization of this hypocrisy that cries out for correction.

Were Police Defending Themselves?

This case draws attention to the disparity. Nathaniel Jones, the victim, had passed out in the parking lot of a White Castle restaurant, doing no physical harm to anyone. Not wanting a man lying on its property, and not employing private guards, the restaurant called the police. The police roused him and an unarmed Jones came up swinging hard. He wasn't complying—the greatest sin in the eyes of the state.

Was he defending himself or were the police defending themselves? It's unclear. What is clear is that he was hit 40 or 50 times with a metal baton (by mostly white police, and one black) before falling and later dying. Traces of PCP were found in his blood and other drugs in his car. The police department is aggressively defending itself against charges of abuse: they say the police obeyed regulations in exacting increasingly hard punishments.

And yet, apart from taking drugs and trespassing, what precisely had Jones done wrong, aside from resisting arrest? The police tried to arrest the guy and one thing led to another until Jones was dead. This is in contrast to the case of Rodney King, whose beating followed not only an attempt to resist arrest but also a dangerous high speed chase in a residential neighborhood that clearly threatened innocents of all sorts. His beating was as much a punishment for this as it was an attempt to restrain.

A Better Approach

In a world in which property owners had absolute rights, what would have happened to Jones? Could the restaurant owner walk up to a passed out man on his private property and blast him in the head? That would be contrary to normal rules of proportionality. . . .

Killing would only be proportional if the person were threatening the life of the owner of the property, or his employees or customers. One can imagine conditions under which a sleeping druggie would go this far, and thereby be due the maximum punishment. But the property owner would have every reason to stop the escalation, if only to avoid legal entanglement and bad publicity.

We should remember that the rules of proportionality set up a maximum allowable punishment but do not mandate it. Good sense suggests that, say, a net or sedative spray might be a better approach when someone resists being thrown off private property. Surely, the police should take this approach, if available, before beating and beating a person until he is dead. In the Rodney King case, the police used stun guns, which had no effect, before resorting to extreme tactics, though, despite appearances, they caused little injury to King. Might this have been a better approach in the Jones case?

Terror Tactics

Our increasingly federalized police seem all too willing in these days of the War on Terror to employ terror tactics whenever they can get away with it. They have been unleashed as never before, and hence have an increasingly antagonistic relationship to the citizenry. They are less and less like servants and more and more like masters.

Roadblocks in the US are now common. We think nothing of showing our papers whenever we are asked. The slightest behavior out of the ordinary calls down questions. You have the distinct impression that you have no recourse to law and that your fate is entirely in the arbitrary hands of the state. The armed agents of the state seem to be experiencing a permanent bout of paranoia.

Imagine how private security guards might have handled the matter differently; Wal-Mart, for example, which uses private security. Might they have just helped the man and tried to contact a family member? Might they have sedated him had he become unruly? Or just backed off for a time until the man stopped protesting? Or offered him $20 or a bottle of scotch to go? They would have at least understood that beating, let alone killing, people on company property is bad for business. But the restaurant called government police who believe they can and should use every amount of force they can get away with under the regulations.

Periodical Bibliography

The following articles have been selected to supplement the diverse views presented in this chapter.

Seth D. DuCharme
"The Search for Reasonableness in Use-of-Force Cases: Understanding the Effects of Stress on Perception and Performance," *Fordham Law Review*, May 2002.

Bruce Eggler
"Independent Monitor Urged for New Orleans Police," *New Orleans Times-Picayune*, April 28, 2006.

Robert J. McClory
"Faith and the Power of Persistence: Catholic Citizen Wages Decades-Long Fight to End Police Brutality," *National Catholic Reporter*, July 18, 2003.

Patrick O'Neill
"Activist Reports Rough Treatment at Arrest," *National Catholic Reporter*, December 19, 2003.

Michael J. Pastor
"A Tragedy and a Crime? Amadou Diallo, Specific Intent, and the Federal Prosecution of Civil Rights Violations," *Legislation and Public Policy*, Fall 2002.

Richard G. Schott
"The Role of Race in Law Enforcement: Racial Profiling or Legitimate Use?" *FBI Law Enforcement Bulletin*, November 2001.

Lisa K. Sloman
"Throw a Dog a Suspect: When Using Police Dogs Becomes an Unreasonable Use of Force Under the Fourth Amendment," *Golden Gate University Law Review*, Spring 2004.

Jeffrey Sturgeon
"A Constitutional Right to Reasonable Treatment: Excessive Force and the Plight of Warrantless Arrestees," *Temple Law Review*, Spring 2004.

Silja J. A. Talvi
"The Public Is the Enemy," *Nation*, December 3, 2003.

USA Today
"More Brutality Allegations Lodged Against New Orleans Police," April 6, 2006.

CHAPTER 2

What Factors Cause Police Brutality?

Chapter Preface

Police work does not take place in a cultural vacuum. Law enforcement officers are influenced by the same social standards, stigmas, and stereotypes that define the communities in which they live and work. According to a 2006 report from Amnesty International, this is one of the reasons that lesbian, gay, bisexual, and transgender (LGBT) Americans continue to experience widespread discrimination and violence at the hands of police officers.

Between 2003 and 2005, Amnesty International studied charges of police brutality against members of the LGBT community in four U.S. cities: Chicago, Los Angeles, New York, and San Antonio. Using personal testimonies, surveys, and interviews to gather data, researchers heard from law enforcement agencies, civilian police-review boards, activist groups, lawyers, and LGBT victims of police discrimination, neglect, or outright abuse. In its report *Stonewalled—Still Demanding Respect*, Amnesty International noted that antigay policing takes two distinct forms. One is direct abuse, brutality, and hostility toward LGBT individuals, and the other is a pattern of unresponsiveness that leaves members of the LGBT community vulnerable to homophobic violence and hate crimes perpetrated by civilians.

The abuses cataloged in the report range from verbal harassment and arrests on false or flimsy pretexts, to rape, beatings, and subsequent retaliation against LGBT individuals who file complaints about police mistreatment. The report also criticizes the widespread practice of holding LGBT arrestees in a custody environment that virtually guarantees they will be abused by other detainees.

According to the Amnesty International report, the legal system provides few protections for victims of sexual-orientation-based police misconduct: "There are still some discriminatory laws; but the bigger problem is the discriminatory way in which many laws are applied, which often results in the arrest and detention of individuals just because of their sexual orientation or gender identity." Beyond the letter of the law, says the report, a general undercurrent of cultural bias against gays, lesbians, and transgendered individuals means that most law enforcement agencies and officials are ill equipped or reluctant to implement the training and monitoring systems needed to reduce such discrimination. Even where monitoring programs exist, the heterosexist culture of most law enforcement agencies means that individual officers are often reluctant to report or intervene in situations of antigay abuse or harassment.

Amnesty International suggests that while stricter disciplinary processes and new training programs are needed to address the behavioral aspects of police discrimination against LGBT individuals, there is also a need to recognize that the problem is greater than any particular law enforcement department and its personnel. The report concludes: "The issue of police brutality cannot be tackled without addressing both the pervasive discrimination that LGBT people face, and the social, economic, and cultural marginalization of many within the LGBT community."

Besides drawing attention to the issue of antigay policing in general, Amnesty International also points out that within the LGBT community, those who are the most vulnerable to police hostility and misconduct share another significant at-risk characteristic: they are members of ethnic or racial minorities. The authors in this chapter debate the role of racism and other social biases on the incidence of police brutality and misconduct in American culture.

"Police brutality and misconduct are merely the major contemporary forms of state-sponsored racist violence."

Racism Is a Factor in Police Violence

Sundiata Keita Cha-Jua

In the following viewpoint Sundiata Keita Cha-Jua asserts that police brutality is the current form of state-sanctioned violence against people of color, primarily African Americans. He argues that such violence is deeply ingrained in Western culture, and can be traced through five hundred years of history. Cha-Jua is director of the African American Studies and Research Program at the University of Illinois at Champaign-Urbana and an associate professor of history.

As you read, consider the following questions:

1. What represented the first moment of "capitalist globalism," according to Cha-Jua?

2. Approximately how many African Americans were lynched in the United States between 1882 and 1930, according to the author?

Sundiata Keita Cha-Jua, "Contemporary Police Brutality and Misconduct: A Continuation of the Legacy of Racial Violence," originally printed by the Black Radical Congress, 2001. Reproduced by permission of the author.

3. According to a Department of Justice survey cited by Cha-Jua, what percentage of police admit that fellow officers sometimes or often use "more force than necessary?"

In the late sixties, Janiil Al-Amin (a.k.a. H. Rap Brown) declared, "Violence is as American as cherry pie." Al-Amin's statement underscores the essential role of violence in maintaining systems of racial oppression in the United States. Racist violence was fundamental to the creation of the United States. Moreover, force and violence are not options but necessary to the maintenance of racial oppression. Racist violence is the scaffolding upon which capitalist exploitation and white supremacy are erected. . . .

Over the last 500 years people of color, especially African Americans, have endured a pattern of state-sanctioned violence, and civil and human rights abuse. To enforce capitalist exploitation and racial oppression the government and its police, courts, prisons, and military have beaten, framed, murdered, and executed private persons, and brutally repressed struggles for freedom, justice, and self-determination. It has initiated wars of conquest, launched man-hunts for fugitive slaves, suppressed slave revolts, brutalized demonstrators, and assassinated political dissidents.

Police brutality and misconduct are merely the major contemporary forms of state-sponsored racist violence. Police brutality describes "instances of serious physical or psychological harm to civilians." Contemporary police brutality consists of deadly force, the use of excessive force, and it includes unjustified shooting, fatal choking, and physical assault by law enforcement officers. Police misconduct is inclusive of planting evidence, making untrue statements, filing untrue written reports, condoning untrue statements and/or reports by keeping silent, threatening suspects, arrestees, and witnesses, engaging in illegal activities, and committing perjury.

This statement summarizes the United States' atrocious record of racial repression, specifically state-sponsored violence. . . .

A History of U.S Racist Violence

Historically, racist violence, legal and extralegal, and whether state-sponsored or private, has been used to impose racial oppression and preserve white power and privilege. Racist violence has served five primary purposes:

1. To force people of color into indentured, slave, peonage, or low-wage situations;
2. To steal land, minerals, and other resources;
3. To maintain social control and to repress rebellions;
4. To restrict or eliminate competition in employment, business, politics, and social life; and
5. To unite "whites" across ethnic/national, class, and gender lines.

Domination of people of color necessitated the incorporation and justification of racially motivated and differentiated violence in the society's law, custom, and popular culture.

Federal, state, and municipal law sanctioned the slave trade, genocidal wars of conquest, slavery, and the brutalities inherent in labor exploitation and racial oppression. Genocide and other forms of government-sponsored or sanctioned violence have been inflicted upon Native Americans since the country's beginning. Latino/a people have been the victims of government-sponsored or sanctioned violence since the U.S. unleashed a colonial war of aggression against the Mexicano people in the middle of the 19th century. Chinese (and later other Asian Americans) have been assaulted by government-sponsored or -sanctioned violence since the middle of the 19th century. Moreover, all branches of government have engaged in violence against workers across color and gender lines or abdicated their equal protection responsibilities during labor disputes.

Systematic Suppression

State-sponsored and state-sanctioned violence has characterized the Black experience since Africans' forced migration to these shores. The Atlantic Slave Trade represented the first moment of capitalist globalism. The slave trade was the first international industry; it was a business venture of European nation-states. Orderly commodity exchange cloaked the coercion and disorder undergirding the Atlantic Slave Trade. Raids and kidnapping were the lifeblood of the slave "trade." About two-thirds of the nearly 12 million Africans enslaved in the Americas were captured through rapacious raids and kidnapping. During the four centuries the slave trade operated, 100 million Africans may have died from the predatory commercial wars launched by European royalty, the papacy, and emerging European and American capitalists.

British colonial and American governments systematically suppressed Africans' human rights. Colonial governments enacted special "slave codes" that legalized physical abuse—whipping—and authored practices that condoned maiming, rape, and murder. After the revolution, individual states preserved and refined antiblack laws, with the support of the federal government. For its part, the new national government enshrined African American slavery into the U.S. Constitution (Article I, sec. 2) and authorized law-enforcement agents to assist in the capture and return of fugitive slaves (Article 4, sec. 2 and the Fugitive Slave Act of 1793).

Racist violence reached its apogee after Emancipation. Lynching, the major form of violence used against African Americans, from 1882–1910, resulted from the encouragement of law enforcement agents or their abdicating their equal protection responsibilities. Between 1882 and 1930 approximately

Police as the Force of the White World

The only way to police a ghetto is to be oppressive. . . . [The police] represent the force of the white world, and that world's criminal profit and ease, to keep the black man corralled up here, in his place. The badge, the gun in the holster, and the swinging club make vivid what will happen should his rebellion become overt. . . . He moves through Harlem, therefore, like an occupying soldier in a bitterly hostile country, which is precisely what, and where, he is, and the reason he walks in twos and threes.

James Baldwin, Nobody Knows My Name, *1962.*

3,000 Blacks (mostly male) were lynched. During the First Nadir (1877–1917), organized gang rape of Black women by white racist mobs and organizations like the Ku Klux Klan was a special form of terrorism reserved for Blacks.

Social Control

After 1930, extralegal race riots and legal executions replaced lynching as means of social control. All white or predominately white juries and government officials merely extended societal racial discrimination to executions. More than half (53%) of the 4,220 persons executed between 1930 and 1996 were Black. Despite the history of white men sexually assaulting Black women, 405 or 90 percent of the 455 men executed for rape between 1930 and 1976 were Black. In 1972 the death penalty was outlawed partly because of its racist and class discriminatory implementation. Since its return in 1976, executions have adhered to their previous racist and class-biased patterns. Thus, people of color have comprised 45 percent or 308 of the 679 executions in the U.S. Two hundred and forty-seven or 36 percent of those executed have been Black. Currently, Blacks on death row are nearly three times their percentage in the overall population (36% to 13%).

The government also bears the responsibility for the actions and non-actions of police officers during race riots and rebellions. Abdication of responsibility coupled with acts of outright brutality and misconduct by law enforcement officers enabled hundreds of race riots (violent clashes between private white and Black citizens) throughout the nation's history. Police brutality or misconduct has been the "trigger incident" that sparked almost every modern rebellion from the 1935 "Harlem Riot" to the 1992 LA Conflagration. For instance, after the beating of Lino Riveria, a Puerto Rican youth by New York City police in 1935, three Blacks were killed, 57 people were injured and $2 million dollars' worth of property was destroyed in Harlem. A patrolman's attack on Marquette Frye sparked an uprising in the [Los Angeles neighborhood of] Watts in 1965. The conflict resulted in hundreds of injuries, 34 deaths, and the damage or destruction of $35 million worth of property. The savage police beating of Arthur McDuffie, a 33-year-old Black insurance executive triggered the 1980 Miami Rebellion. The 1992 LA Rebellion was a response to the March 3, 1991 brutalizing of Rodney G. King by three LA police officers. Twenty-three other law enforcement officers watched as King was beaten, kicked and shocked by officers wielding batons and stun guns.

In contemporary America, police brutality is the preferred form of social control. Several local, state, and federal commissions, particularly the 1967 National Advisory Commission on Civil Disorders (the Kerner Commission) have pointed out the immensity of this problem. The police are, as the Black Panther Party declared in the 1960s, "an occupying army of repression."

Police Brutality

Police brutality has been a persistent problem faced by African Americans. The failure of government to protect Black people

Kirk Anderson. Reproduced by permission.

from lawless law enforcement officers forced Blacks to act in their own interests. During the 1930s, the National Negro Congress [NNC] organized massive rallies against this form of terror. In Washington, D.C., over the span of a few months, the NNC collected 24,000 signatures protesting abuse by the D.C. police department. The Black Panther Party was created to stem the tide of police abuse. In the 1970s the Congress of Afrikan Peoples sponsored the "Stop Killer Cops" Campaigns. Extralegal violence by law enforcement officers has been a primary concern of the Congressional Black Caucus [CBC] since its formation. The CBC has periodically held public hearings about police outrages across the country over the last thirty years. Yet, extralegal violence persists as recent police killings of Richard L. Holtz (Fort Lee, New Jersey); Tynisha Miller (Riverside, California); and Amadou Diallo (New York City) attest.

Finally, police administrators have ignored or been lax in using internal department policies and procedures to punish officers who have displayed a pattern of brutality and/or misconduct. Internal department policies are often weak, and internal investigations are generally conducted poorly. A Justice Department survey found that nearly 22 percent of police admit that fellow officers sometimes or often use "more force than necessary". Moreover, 61 percent claimed officers do not report instances of "serious criminal violations of abuse of authority" by other officers. Civilian review boards are generally underfunded and lack the legal authority to compel police officers' participation, nor can they enforce findings. To date, private civil suits have yet to demonstrate the capacity to reform individual or police departmental behavior because they do not address the policies and procedures of departments. Although the Violent Crime Control and Law Enforcement Act of 1994 authorized the Civil Rights Division of the Department of Justice to bring "civil actions" against police departments that evidence a pattern of abuse, they also have not deterred the continuation of police brutality and misconduct. Moreover, neither the offending officer nor the department is held financially liable for judgements. Finally, criminal prosecutions for police brutality or misconduct rarely occur because few state prosecutors are willing to aggressively pursue abusive officers. This pattern is also true for federal prosecutors, although to a lesser extent.

Force of Arms Not Law

We believe that existing local, county, state, and federal policies and laws have been ineffective in ending the persistent and pervasive practices of police brutality and misconduct. Moreover, we believe that because police officers operate under "color of law" that civil and human rights violations committed by officers undermine respect for law and government. Furthermore, we believe the logical consequence of police violence and misconduct is a society ruled by the force of arms, not law. Thus, every act of police brutality and misconduct, every frame-up, every act of illegal surveillance, every "justified" murder erases an article from the Bill of Rights and takes us another step closer to a police state.

> "Statistics that tabulate officer-civilian interactions by race alone grossly distort the reality of policing, many black cops complain."

The Police Are Not Racist

Heather Mac Donald

In the following viewpoint Heather Mac Donald cites several African American police officers who share her belief that the police are not racist. According to her, the police target blacks more than whites because more blacks commit crimes. The black officers that Mac Donald interviewed say that charges of racism undermine the good work of police departments across the nation. Mac Donald is a fellow at the Manhattan Institute, a social-policy organization that works to foster greater economic choice and individual responsibility. She is a well-known media commentator and writer on homeland security and policing issues.

As you read, consider the following questions:

1. How do "racial politics" affect black progress, in Mac Donald's opinion?
2. Of the officers that Mac Donald spoke to, did most accept or reject what she calls the "racial profiling myth?"

Heather Mac Donald, "Black and True Blue," *New York Daily News*, July 14, 2002. Reproduced by permission of the author.

3. Who are constantly attacking the "moral authority" of the police, according to the author?

Ask Detective Carl McLaughlin whether the police prey on black people, and this normally ebullient Brooklyn cop will respond icily, "I just prey on people that are preying on others. It shouldn't be a race thing."

A cop's denial that policing is racist is perhaps not note-worthy—except for one thing: McLaughlin is black. As such, he represents an ignored constituency in contemporary polic-ing controversies: black officers who loathe race-based cop-bashing as much as any Irish flatfoot.

As the American Civil Liberties Union and other profes-sional cop haters flood the media with tales of endemic police racism, rank-and-file minority officers, who might be consid-ered ideal commentators on these matters, appear only as in-triguing statistics—such as those showing that black state troopers in New Jersey, the alleged cradle of racial profiling, stop the same proportion of black drivers as do their purport-edly racist white colleagues.

Anti-Cop Propaganda

So I set out and talked to several dozen black cops and com-manders from eight police departments, from Brooklyn to Olympia, Wash., about why they became police officers and how they view today's policing controversies. What I found was a bracing commitment to law and order, a resounding re-jection of anti-cop propaganda and a conviction that racial politics are a tragic drag on black progress.

The thoroughly mainstream views of these black cops are a reminder that invisible behind the antics of Al Sharpton and Jesse Jackson are many black citizens who share the common-sense values of most Americans.

This is not to excuse the manhandling of the handcuffed suspect [Donovan Jackson in Los Angeles in July 2003]. But

Steve Kelley. © 1995 Steve Kelley, *The San Diego Union-Tribune*. Reprinted with permission.

while anomalies like that make headlines, the everyday dedication of officers, black and white, is treated as not news.

All black officers, whatever their reason for joining the force, face the same occupational hazard race-based taunting. "You work for 'The Man'" McLaughlin constantly hears in Brooklyn. "I don't work for 'The Man'" he says impatiently. "I work for the penal law."

Policing Is an Imperative

It is their emotional relation to the good people of the community that makes policing such an imperative for these cops. Many come from God-fearing, law-abiding homes where respect for authority was absolute. These officers have seen firsthand the damage done by thugs, and they are determined to stop it. "I will never retreat," vows McLaughlin. "We are the last line of defense against mayhem."

Amid all the anti-cop taunting they hear, they remind themselves, in the words of Officer David Brown, that crime victims "regard you as heroes."

If the law-abiding black poor and middle class are no abstractions for these cops—as they are for guilty white liberals, who condescendingly think they are benefiting black people by promoting criminal-friendly policies—neither is the depravity of young thugs some distant construct to be brushed away for the more gratifying exercise of understanding the underprivileged.

Constant exposure to criminals teaches cops how to recognize them. "Just as we stand out, they stand out," explains Officer Troy Smith of San Antonio, Tex. But being black by no means insulates officers from the racial profiling charge when they arrest a lowlife they've spotted.

Most officers I spoke to reject the racial profiling myth. If you're stopped, they said, it's for a reason—you fit a description or you've done something to raise an officer's suspicion, such as hitch up your waistband in a way that suggests a hidden gun. Statistics that tabulate officer-civilian interactions by race alone grossly distort the reality of policing, many black cops complain.

Unless top management reassures cops that they can count on support in strong enforcement actions, black officers caution, some cops will inevitably back off in the face of racial pressures.

Cops—black, white, Hispanic, you name it—scratch their heads at the seeming priorities of the so-called community. "There can be 50 shootings [by] civilians, and no one will protest," marvels John Hayward, a fast-talking community-response officer from the Philadelphia department. "If a cop shoots one person, everyone's demonstrating. If you protest against us, why don't you protest against the drug dealers?"

Policing Should Not Be a Racial Transaction

Cops do not merely arrest people, they enforce social norms where social norms are the least entrenched and the most needed. In my dad's old neighborhood, a cop was often more likely to slap a kid around than actually press charges for something like shoplifting (my dad was a good boy and did no such thing, FYI). The slapping was surely just as illegal then as it is now, but the intent was consistent with the hidden law [unwritten norms that regulate everyday behavior]. . . .

Indeed, to me it's a tragedy that a white cop can't give a black kid a kick in the pants without it automatically being interpreted by the kid and the community as a racial transaction. A lot of good kids have probably been thrown into the "system" because white cops were reluctant to treat them the same way they would treat a white kid.

Jonah Goldberg, National Review Online, *January 17, 2000. www.nationalreviewonline.com.*

Moral Authority Is Under Siege

Surely the cops would get more support from the community if their moral authority were not constantly under siege from left-wing activists within and outside police departments. Lt. Eric Adams of the NYPD [New York Police Department] has made a media career for himself by testifying against the department before every camera he can find, as the self-appointed head of a mysterious organization called One Hundred Blacks in Law Enforcement Who Care.

Every time Adams says something negative about the police, observes Wilbur Chapman, the NYPD's chief of patrol during the 1990s, the department loses blacks who are "on the fence," whether as witnesses or potential recruits. "There's no voice to say, 'This is not the reality,'" says Chapman. (Adams did not return my calls.)

The sum total of these pressures is a police force fighting with one hand tied behind its back, according to many black officers—contrary to black activists who incessantly portray police force as out of control.

Sadly, the media and politicians never recognize these moderate voices as valid representatives of black officers. The perverse logic of race politics, even within police departments, dictates that the only authentic blacks are angry blacks. And so the supposed spokesmen for black officers are almost always the most radical members of a department, usually unelected, who push a grievance agenda of quotas and lower standards.

The long-running race racket that has so distorted our national discourse shows no signs of letting up, but that is only because we have been listening to the wrong people. There is no inherent reason why only the victimologists should be granted legitimacy as representatives of black interests, especially since so few of them are elected.

Why not at least give equal time to a Wilbur Chapman, say, when he argues that the "biggest impediment to minority advancement is white guilt" and asserts that, whatever the remaining problems in American race relations, "the bottom line is: No one can stop me from getting my piece of the American dream"?

Support for Law Enforcement

As for the state of policing itself, while my interlocutors don't constitute a perfectly constructed, randomized sample, neither do Adams and his counterparts across the country. And, unlike the cop complainers, these pro-police cops are not seeking benefits or power from their testimony.

I believe that the support for law enforcement expressed by these officers is widespread among black cops. Their voices represent an essential, and wholly overlooked, perspective on current law enforcement controversies, one that should give us hope not just about the politics of policing, but about race relations writ large.

> "Alberta Spruill's tragic death is a dramatic example of the evil consequences that result from . . . the increasing militarization of this country's police."

The Militarization of Law Enforcement Causes Police Brutality

Donald E. Wilkes Jr.

In the following viewpoint Donald E. Wilkes Jr. maintains that police increasingly are adopting militaristic tactics in their everyday activities and that citizens are being brutalized as a result. He focuses on the dangers of "no-knock" entries and the use of stun grenades during police raids on citizens to show how police are acting like soldiers. Wilkes condemns the militarization of the police, pointing out that citizens are not enemies to be defeated but people protected by the Bill of Rights. A prolific author on legal issues, Wilkes is a professor at the University of Georgia School of Law.

Donald E. Wilkes Jr., "Explosive Dynamic Entry: The Increasing Militarization of the Police Makes Citizens into Enemies," *Flagpole Magazine*, July 30, 2003, p. 8. Reproduced by permission.

As you read, consider the following questions:

1. What are three examples of military equipment being used more and more commonly by police, according to information cited by Wilkes?

2. In what year were stun grenades deployed for the first time by police, as reported by Wilkes?

3. How many other people were slain by American police using stun grenades to carry out a search warrant prior to the death of Alberta Spruill, according to the author?

At 6 A.M., on Friday, May 16, 2003, 57-year-old Alberta Spruill was in her residence, Apartment 6F at 310 W. 143rd Street in the Harlem section of New York City, preparing to leave for work. Spruill, a quiet, church-going woman, was a municipal worker, employed at the Division of Citywide Administrative Services. She had been a city employee for 29 years, and each weekday would take the bus to her job. To her, that Friday morning must have seemed like the beginning of just another ordinary day. She mercifully did not know that she would never again head for work, that she had in fact but two hours to live because she was soon to be killed by the police even though she was an innocent citizen.

Scared to Death

Ten minutes later a dozen heavily armed police—six officers from the Emergency Service Unit and six regular patrol officers—burst unannounced into her residence. They had a search warrant issued solely on the basis of erroneous information supplied by an unreliable anonymous informer who falsely claimed that illegal guns and drugs were stored at Spruill's residence, that he had seen armed individuals there on three occasions, and that there were dogs inside. First the officers suddenly broke down the front door with a battering ram. Then they heaved a stun grenade into the apartment where it exploded with a blinding white flash, a deafening bang, and a thunderous concussion. Then they stormed in and handcuffed Spruill, placing her face down on the floor. She was coughing and screaming. Spruill, who suffered from high blood pressure, then began having difficulty breathing. An ambulance for Spruill was dispatched at 6:32 A.M. When Spruill arrived at Harlem Hospital at 8 A.M. she was pronounced dead. She had suffered a fatal heart attack.

The medical examiner performed an autopsy and announced that Spruill suffered "sudden death following a police raid" as a result of shock and fear caused by the stun grenade explosion and the stress of being handcuffed. The medical examiner also officially classified Spruill's death a homicide—a death caused by another person's actions. "She really was scared to death," a New York newspaper wrote the day after the medical examiner's announcement.

Alberta Spruill's tragic death is a dramatic example of the evil consequences that result from an extremely ominous development in American policing—the increasing militarization of this country's police. Militarizing the police "can lead to dangerous . . . consequences—such as unnecessary shootings and killings," Diane Cecilia Weber, a criminal justice expert authority, observed [in 1999]. The killing of Spruill is powerful confirmation of Ms. Weber's observation.

"Militarization," according to sociologist Timothy J. Dunn, author of a 1996 book on the militarizing of American law enforcement agencies, "refers to the use of military rhetoric and ideology, as well as military tactics, strategy, technology, equipment, and forces." The leading scholarly paper on the militarization of American law enforcement is Diane Cecilia Weber's *Warrior Cops: The Ominous Growth of Paramilitarism in American Police Departments* (1999). The two most alarming side effects of this militarization of the police, we learn from Ms. Weber's study, are: (1) "state and local police officers are increasingly emulating the war-fighting tactics of soldiers," and (2) "a culture of paramilitarism . . . currently pervades many . . . police departments."

Helmets and Combat Boots

Ms. Weber gives numerous examples of how "state and local police departments are increasingly accepting the military as the model for their behavior," and "increasingly emulating the tactics of the armed forces in their everyday activities." Police are now using more and more military equipment. "Between 1995 and 1997 the Department of Defense gave police departments 1.2 million pieces of military hardware," including armored personnel carriers, grenade launchers, submachine guns, and explosive devices. SWAT teams resembling the military's special forces have proliferated, organized like military units with "a commander, a tactical team leader, a scout, a rear guard, a sniper, a spotter, a gas man, and paramedics." (Recently some SWAT teams have been given more euphemistic designations, e.g., Emergency Response Team, Special Response Team, Special Emergency Response Team, Tactical Response Team, Emergency Services Unit, and Strategic Operations Group.) "[A]bout half of SWAT members get their training from active-duty military personnel, some of them from the Navy SEALS or Army Rangers." Equipped with military-style weapons such as submachine guns with laser sights and sound suppressors, members of police SWAT teams dress in such a way that they are difficult to distinguish from combat soldiers. SWAT police wear black or dark battle dress uniforms, or military or camouflage fatigues; they have metal or Kevlar helmets; they wear masks or hoods; they have protective goggles over their eyes; they wear full body armor; Nomex gloves cover their hands; they often carry a bunker (a large bullet-proof shield with a small window through which the officer looks); and they are shod in laced combat boots. Originally designed to deal with hijackings, hostage-takings, and other emergency situations, SWAT teams are increasingly involved in routine policing duties; "today," according to Ms. Weber, "these special forces are deployed three-quarters of the time in 'warrant work,'" i.e., executing arrest and search warrants, usually in drug cases. "The SWAT modus operandi—the quick, violent, military-style confrontation . . . has become normalized in police departments" across America. This explains why three criminologists, in their authoritative treatise on police lawlessness, *Forces of Deviance: Understanding the Dark Side of Policing* (1998), caustically comment that for American police today "[t]he training orientation often resembles preparation for being dropped behind enemy lines on a combat mission."

"[T]he last several decades," journalist Tom Baxter notes, "[have] brought not only military equipment but a military mindset into the realm of domestic law enforcement." Ms. Weber's treatise provides numerous examples of how police militarization has "spawned a culture of paramilitarism in American law enforcement," and has resulted in too many "state and local police officers adopting the . . . mindset of their military mentors." When law enforcement officials develop a "military mindset," when they begin to view themselves as "warrior police," individual rights are seriously jeopardized. It means "an organizational culture that [leads police] to escalate situations upward rather than de-escalating." As Ms. Weber explains: "The problem is that the mindset of the soldier is not appropriate for the civilian police officer. Police officers confront not an 'enemy' but individuals who are protected by the Bill of Rights. . . . The job of a police officer is to keep the peace, but not by just any means. Police officers are expected to apprehend suspected lawbreakers while adhering to constitutional protections. They are expected to use *minimum* force and to deliver suspects to a court of law. The soldier, on the other hand, is an instrument of war. If [police] have a mindset that the goal is to take out a citizen, it will happen. . . . Blending military and civilian law enforcement is dangerous because the mindset of the police officer is not— and should not be—that of a warrior. The job of the police is to apprehend a *suspect*—nearly always a fellow American citi-

No Respect

It is still not clear exactly what happened after police entered Miss Alberta's apartment. They claim they were looking for a drug dealer and that as soon as they realized they had the wrong apartment, they immediately uncuffed Alberta Spruill.

But neighbors tell a different story. Belica Rivera told *Newsday*, "She was crying. She was coughing. She said, 'I can't breathe. My chest hurts. I can't breathe.'" Rivera says she saw Miss Alberta in the hallway handcuffed a half hour after police busted in. Another woman told the [*Revolutionary Worker*], "My sister was frightened by the noise. She lives down the hall and she opened her door to see. They told her to close her door and get in her house—like she's a criminal. There's no respect at all. They feel that anybody that's in our area is a drug dealer, drug user, drug pusher. And it doesn't go that way. She worked for the same city that killed her."

Revolutionary Worker, *June 1, 2003. www.rwor.org.*

zen—while adhering to constitutional procedures.... A soldier, however, is an instrument of war, and war is the use of unrestrained force against an *enemy* ... often by inflicting maximum damage.... [A] soldier with a machine gun doesn't worry about *Miranda rights.*"

"Dynamic Entry"

The changes in actual police practices resulting from militarization are observable in almost every aspect of police work, but it is probably in regard to search and seizure practices that these changes are most strikingly obvious. A good example involves the methods used to effect entry into residences to execute search warrants. Over the course of the last three decades such entries more and more have come to resemble military commando operations. It is now a standard practice throughout this land for SWAT teams or other large squads of heavily armed police serving search or arrest warrants to smash front doors with battering rams and rush in with guns drawn, barking out orders and forcing everyone inside to "prone out" and submit to handcuffing in the back—all without first giving the occupants notice of the police presence or an opportunity to open the door. The police-created euphemism for this increasingly common form of no-knock entry into residences is "dynamic entry." Furthermore, over the last two decades the militarized police units carrying out dynamic entries have increasingly resorted to the use of explosive devices when making such entries. It is now a not uncommon practice for police effecting no-knock entry to detonate stun grenades in residences after they have broken open a door or window but prior to their actually entering the premises. This, of course, is exactly what happened in Alberta Spruill's case. She was a victim of what might be called "explosive dynamic entry."

Stun grenades were introduced into the arsenal of American police agencies, and deployed for the first time, by Los Angeles, California, police in 1982. Although there can be no doubt that the police tactic of using stun grenades to serve warrants on residences has been steadily increasing, or that the grenades are now used for this purpose by police throughout the United States, it is difficult to obtain reliable statistical information on the matter. (This is unsurprising. Although the government collects and disseminates gigabytes of statistics on crimes or acts of violence committed by citizens against other citizens, or by citizens against police, there are hardly any official statistics on crimes or acts of violence committed against citizens by police. Crime statistics do not, for example, tell us how many people are shot or clubbed or Maced by police, or suffer injuries while being arrested or while in police custody, or are subjected to a chokehold or fingerhold, or bitten by a police dog.) A 1987 California Supreme Court decision discloses that in 1985 the Los Angeles police deployed stun grenades on 25 occasions, and following Alberta Spruill's killing New York City police announced that while executing search warrants in the late 1990's the Emergency Service Unit used stun grenades 50 to 75 times a year, 66 times in 2000, 129 times in 2001, and 152 times in 2002. Between Jan. 1 and May 16, 2003, it used stun grenades to serve warrants 85 times. It seems indisputable that during the past 20 years police have effected hundreds, perhaps even thousands, of explosive dynamic entries all over the country and that [from 1998 to 2003] there have been more such entries than in all previous years.

A Bang and a Flash

A stun grenade, unlike the traditional grenade, the purpose of which is to kill or wound, is designed to stun and distract by producing a temporarily blinding light and a temporarily deafening concussion, but without the propulsion or dispersion of shrapnel. A stun grenade produces a sensory overload with a loud bang and a brilliant flash which disorients and confuses persons nearby. It also produces smoke. Stun grenades carry a warning label that misuse can cause physical injury or death.

To downplay the sinister police-state implications of their growing use of these explosive devices, police refuse to call them stun grenades, preferring to use euphemisms such as "flash bangs," "distractionary devices," "diversionary devices," "cylindrical pyrotechnical devices," or even "a type of firecracker." In 2000, however, a federal court of appeals vigorously expressed its disdain for both these linguistic affectations and the increasing police use of stun grenades, remarking that "police cannot automatically throw bombs into the drug dealers' houses, even if the bomb goes by the euphemism 'flash bang device.'"

Stun grenades are regarded as nonlethal weapons, but they are inherently dangerous and can, as the killing of Alberta Spruill proves, cause death. "The term 'nonlethal' refers to the goal which is to avoid fatalities," Lt. Col. James C. Duncan writes in an article published in the *Naval Law Review* in 1998. "The public should be aware that the use of a nonlethal weapon always raises the possibility of serious injury, death, or destruction of property."

Alberta Spruill was not the first but, at a minimum, the fourth person slain by American police using stun grenades to execute a search warrant. On Dec. 13, 1984, Los Angeles police killed a woman who died of injuries resulting from the explosion of several stun grenades thrown into the room of her residence where she was watching television, and on Jan. 25, 1989, an elderly couple in Minneapolis, Minnesota, died in bed of smoke inhalation after police threw a stun grenade through a window in their residence, starting a fire.

Recklessness

From 1987 through May 2003 there have been at least 27 reported appellate court decisions—15 in the federal courts, 12 in the state courts—involving police detonation of one or more stun grenades to serve a warrant in 19 states and the District of Columbia. In all but two of these cases the stun grenades were deployed by state or local police rather than federal agents. All the cases involved search warrants for drugs, or for drugs and firearms. In five of the 27 cases the explosion inflicted a nonfatal injury on one of the occupants, and in four other cases it caused property damage. In six of the 27 cases more than one stun grenade was detonated. The time of the explosive dynamic entry is given in 15 of the 27 cases. In only four of these cases did the entry occur between 8:30 a.m.

and 8:30 p.m. In 11 of the 15 cases the entry occurred either late at night or very early in the morning. In six cases the entry occurred between 10 p.m. and 3:25 a.m., and in the remaining five cases the entry was between 6:09 a.m. and 7 a.m.

The factual scenarios of these cases show how rashly and recklessly police sometimes act in using stun grenades for purposes of dynamic entry. They throw exploding stun grenades through doorways and windows into living rooms, bedrooms, kitchens, and basements. They throw exploding stun grenades into rooms without first checking to see who is in the room or who is present in the residence. They throw exploding stun grenades into rooms or residences where they know or should know innocent women, children, and babies are present. They throw stun grenades which explode on or near people and inflict physical injuries. They throw exploding stun grenades into bedrooms where small children are present. They throw exploding stun grenades which land in baby strollers from which a baby had been removed a few minutes earlier. They throw exploding stun grenades which burn furniture, rugs, and floors, and which start fires.

The 27 appellate decisions indicate that, while courts sometimes do express concern about police use of exploding devices to serve warrants, legal attacks on the validity of explosive dynamic entry raids are likely to be unsuccessful. Nineteen of the cases involved appeals from criminal convictions, and only in one instance did the court reverse a conviction on grounds the entry violated the Fourth Amendment. Seven of the 27 cases involved civil actions for damages in behalf of persons subjected to an explosive dynamic entry; in not a single instance did the appellate court uphold or enter a monetary judgment in favor of a plaintiff. Such is the moribund condition of judicial protection of Fourth Amendment rights in an era of law and order judges, public apathy about constitutional criminal procedure protections, martial rhetoric about the war on crime and drugs, and police agencies imbued with a military mentality and equipped with military accouterments and appurtenances.

Bombs Away

It is not the purpose of this [viewpoint] to argue that police should never at any time use stun grenades. There may be exceptional, extraordinary circumstances involving terrorists, hostage-taking, barricaded suspects, or violent mentally deranged people where deployment of stun grenades is appropriate. The threat to liberty lies not in the infrequent use of these weapons on certain special occasions, but in the growing likelihood that use of these explosive devices may be routinized and become a standard and permanent aspect of normal police practices such as the serving of warrants. Explosive dynamic entry, a Gestapo-like tactic, must not and cannot be allowed to become, in the words of Diane Cecilia Weber, "a part of everyday law enforcement in a free society." Otherwise there will be more Alberta Spruills.

"Democracy," Winston Churchill once wrote, "means that if the door bell rings in the early hours, it is likely to be the milkman." America, however, appears to be moving into a warrior police regime where there is no ring of the door bell, and it is not the milkman who is at the door early in the morning; it is a squad of bomb-tossing policemen who think, act and look like military commandos, who are about to burst into the home with no prior warning, and whose motto has become: "To Serve and Protect. Bombs Away!"

> "Advocates say different police tactics could greatly reduce the likelihood of violence [against the mentally ill]."

Ineffective Handling of the Mentally Ill Causes Police Brutality

Adelle Waldman

In the following viewpoint journalist Adelle Waldman describes the violence that can result when police confront mentally ill citizens. Such situations occur more frequently today, she contends, because fewer mentally ill people reside in hospitals and more live on the streets. She points to the need for more extensive police training in the most effective ways to handle people with mental illnesses, as well as better tracking and treatment of emotionally disturbed persons.

As you read, consider the following questions:

1. How many more mentally ill people are on the streets today than in the 1960s, according to Waldman?

2. What does the author say *EDP* stand fors in police parlance?

Adelle Waldman, "Police Struggle with Approach to the Mentally Ill," *Christian Science Monitor*, March 17, 2004. Reproduced by permission of the author.

3. How many times in a year do the New York City police deal with mentally ill people, according to Waldman?

Loretta Cerbelli lost her son Kevin six years ago when the delusional 30-year-old walked into a police station in New York's borough of Queens and stabbed an officer without provocation. Less than two minutes later, other officers shot him to death.

Sue Nickerson lost her son three years ago. A police officer in Centreville, Md., Michael Nickerson answered a call about a noise disturbance in a trailer park and was shot and killed by a mentally ill man.

It seems unlikely that the mother of a slain officer—whose surviving son is also a police officer—and the mother of a man killed at the hands of police would see eye to eye.

But in different states and by different means, Loretta Cerbelli and Sue Nickerson are fighting for a common cause: Both want better tracking and treatment of the mentally ill and more training for police officers who deal with them. "Police officers should be on alert when they get a call" concerning someone who is mentally ill, says Ms. Nickerson, head of the Maryland chapter of Concerns of Police Survivors. "Then maybe they could defuse the situation."

In Philadelphia [in February 2004], Julio Morais clashed with officers who were called to his apartment to help commit him to a mental hospital. Mr. Morais stabbed an officer and was subsequently shot in the head. It was the third time in six months that a mentally ill person was killed by Philadelphia police. Just before Christmas [2003], officers shot and killed a woman who had been running naked down a street and who had come at them with a knife.

These deaths might have been avoided if police had been better trained, says Susan Rogers, director of special projects for the Mental Health Association of Southeastern Pennsylvania.

Police—Not Hospitals—Deal with Mentally Ill

The evidence is overwhelming that the criminal justice system is shouldering much of the burden once carried by hospitals that cared for mentally ill people. Randy Borum, PsyD, who teaches mental health law and policy at the University of South Florida, notes that while in 1955 some 0.3% of Americans were in mental hospitals, today that same percentage of mentally ill people are in the prison system.

And in big cities, he says, as many as 7% of police calls involve the mentally ill. . . .

Experts say one reason such calls are so difficult for police is that most of their training has been in dealing with criminals who generally respond more rationally—dropping a weapon on an officer's command, for example—than a suspect who is emotionally disturbed.

Kathy Bunch, "When Cops Confront Mental Illness," 2001.
www.medicinenet.com.

"Police officers don't want to kill the mentally ill," Ms. Rogers says. "They are responding out of fear."

Although the Philadelphia Police Department did not return calls for this story, officers have said that the killings appear to have been justified.

Such shootings occur around the country with a frequency that alarms advocates of the mentally ill.

In part, it's because more mentally ill people are on the streets than ever before—500,000 more today than there were in the 1960s, when it was easier to commit them to institutions, says James Fyfe, deputy commissioner for training with the New York Police Department. Mr. Fyfe says NYPD [New

York Police Department] dispatchers take a call from an emotionally disturbed person, or an EDP in police lingo, every 7.3 minutes.

People on both sides agree these individuals can be as dangerous to the public and police officers as rational criminals. But advocates say different police tactics could greatly reduce the likelihood of violence.

Much of what police officers are trained to do in dealing with rational criminals is dangerously wrong when it comes to the mentally ill, said Ron Honberg, legal director of the National Association for the Mentally Ill.

"Closing in on someone, sending out a SWAT team—these are prescriptions for disaster," he says. When officers "learn to keep their distance and talk soothingly, it significantly cuts down the chance of escalation."

Many in law enforcement agree.

Some large cities have trained officers to deal with the mentally ill and work in collaboration with mental health agencies, a model that was pioneered in Memphis, Tenn.

About 225 out of 1,000 Memphis police officers have undergone 40 hours of training. When these officers arrive on a scene involving a mentally ill individual, they are in charge, regardless of rank.

That model has been adopted in Houston and Portland, Ore., and is lauded by many advocates.

"It's not that with the Memphis model there will never again be another tragedy," Rogers says. "But there will be fewer tragedies."

Not everyone agrees that the Memphis model is the best way.

Fyfe of the New York Police Department says it wouldn't be appropriate in his city, where the police have 150,000 dealings with the mentally ill a year, compared to about 18,000 in Memphis.

The vast majority of situations that end violently begin to go awry in the first 30 or 40 seconds after police arrive, he says. Rather than train a special squad, "it is much more important to raise the level of expertise of first responders," Fyfe says.

So, [in 2002], the NYPD added two chapters on dealing with the mentally ill to the textbook for new recruits and added extensive role-playing exercises to its training.

And Fyfe says the department does a pretty good job.

"In 2002, we shot four EDPs [out] of 150,000 calls," he says.

In two of those cases, the person shot had first stabbed an officer, he said. "Find me a profession with better professional performance," he says.

It's not good enough for Loretta Cerbelli. Cerbelli, whose son Kevin was killed in 1998, has sued the NYPD for $90 million and policy changes, including revising guidelines that recommend encircling the target in a "zone of safety."

Kevin Cerbelli had been treated for schizophrenia for years. In October 1998, he entered a police station, carrying a knife, a screwdriver, and a rosary, and allegedly used the screwdriver to stab an officer who held open the door for him.

Officers then surrounded Cerbelli and told him to drop the weapons. They tried to subdue him with a nonlethal Taser gun, which sends a jolt of electricity and is supposed to temporarily immobilize suspects, but it didn't seem to affect Cerbelli.

So they shot him.

"It's totally unacceptable that this could have happenend in a police station," Ms. Cerbelli says. "My son should be alive today."

That's how Sue Nickerson feels, too. But she knows just how dangerous an erratic, mentally ill person can be to police officers.

In February 2001, her son and another officer answered a complaint that Frank Zito, who had been diagnosed with schizophrenic and bipolar disorders, was playing music too loudly.

When he would not turn down the music or let the officers into his trailer, they tried to force their way in. Then Zito allegedly shot and killed them.

He has since been convicted and executed for the murders.

But Zito should have been living in a mental health facility or at least made to take his medication, Nickerson says.

She would like to see better coordination between police and mental-health agencies to ensure that people who are dangerous are off the streets.

And she is frustrated that the privacy rights of the mentally ill often get in the way of such coordination.

"Frank Zito pulled the trigger that killed my son," she says. "But perhaps the system helped him load it."

Periodical Bibliography

The following articles have been selected to supplement the diverse views presented in this chapter.

American Civil
Liberties Union of
New Jersey
"ACLU-NJ Requests Review of Discrimination Against Gays at Park," July 27, 2005. www.aclu-nj.org.

Amnesty International
"Police Mistreatment and Abuse Widespread in Lesbian, Gay, Bisexual and Transgender Communities Nationwide," September 22, 2005. www.amnestyusa.org.

Michelle Chen
"Amnesty Cites Systemic Causes of Anti-gay Policing," *NewStandard*, March 24, 2006.

William Norman
Grigg
"Militarizing Mayberry," *New American*, October 7, 2002.

Michael Huspek
"Black Press, White Press, and Their Opposition: The Case of the Police Killing of Tyisha Miller," *Social Justice*, Fall 2004.

Jet
"Controversial Death of Another Black Man in Cincinnati Police Custody Puts City in National Spotlight," December 22, 2003.

Edmund W. Lewis
"Cops Gone Wild," *Louisiana Weekly*, April 10, 2006.

Andrew Murr
"Back on the Mean Streets: A Cop Shoots, a Black Kid Falls and L.A. Is on Edge Again," *Newsweek*, February 21, 2005.

John Pope
"Katrina Took Toll on Emergency Workers," *New Orleans Times-Picayune*, April 28, 2006.

Jonathan D. Silver
"Race Called Key Factor in Police Brutality," *Pittsburgh Post-Gazette*, January 29, 2004.

CHAPTER 3

Does the War on Terror Invite Law-Enforcement Abuses?

Chapter Preface

In the years following the September 11, 2001, al Qaeda attacks on the United States, local police departments inherited new homeland security responsibilities. During the same period, the USA Patriot Act, first approved by Congress in 2001 and renewed in March 2006, lifted some of the restrictions that traditionally governed law enforcement activities such as surveillance, searches of persons or places, and seizure of property and personal data.

As a result, critics are concerned that the War on Terror is placing U.S. civil liberties at risk. In fact, some suggest that the highly publicized abuses that took place at the Abu Ghraib prison in Iraq offer a glimpse at what could occur on U.S. soil, now that the Patriot Act allows law enforcement agencies to engage in previously restricted activity. What possible connection is there between the Patriot Act in the United States and the torture of prisoners overseas?

The Patriot Act grants domestic law enforcement agencies significant tactical latitude in detecting and prosecuting crimes that may be classified as domestic terrorism. In a shadowy parallel, legal opinions drafted by the U.S. Justice Department during the last quarter of 2001 created a secret program that expanded the scope of permissible tactics to be used in the wartime detention and interrogation of international terrorism suspects. The behind-the-scenes plan was designed to sidestep the Geneva Conventions that protect enemy prisoners from torture and the use of excessive force. At first, this was supposed to apply only to Taliban and al Qaeda detainees at Guantánamo Bay; however, a *Newsweek* magazine investigation in 2004 revealed that the success of the secret plan, which had been approved at the highest levels of President George W. Bush's administration, led to a similar suspension of Geneva Conventions protections for detainees in Iraq, as well.

Moreover, no special training or monitoring system was established to oversee this.

In April 2004, the world saw the first horrific photographs of prisoners being intimidated and humiliated by grinning U.S. prison guards at Abu Ghraib. Military and government spokespersons asserted that these acts were committed by rogue personnel, low-ranking soldiers or civilian contractors acting on their own. Eventually, seven soldiers were dishonorably discharged, having been convicted in military trials and sentenced to federal prison time. Other soldiers and officers were removed from duty or demoted.

How might the Abu Ghraib scandal foreshadow brutality and abuse on the part of police in the United States? Typically, when law enforcement authority is expanded, abuses occur as the new boundaries are tested, especially if appropriate training and monitoring systems are not yet available. Arthur Hulnick, a retired military intelligence officer and a veteran of the Central Intelligence Agency, also notes that psychological research reveals that some individuals, if "given a chance where they have total control over someone, will abuse them in some way." Both patterns of behavior are observable in the Abu Ghraib situation and in patterns of police misconduct in the United States.

Even the harshest critics of the Patriot Act do not presume that the specific abuses discovered at Abu Ghraib will be repeated in U.S. jails or prisons. Still, there are concerns that individual rights have eroded due to the War on Terror and that the eventual outcome will be an increase in the abuse of power by law enforcement personnel. The viewpoints in this chapter debate such issues, including delayed-notice searches and their relationship to the War on Terror.

> "The widespread problem of lawlessness in law enforcement ... will simply become exacerbated under a system where police learn at the police academy how to clandestinely burglarize the premises of Americans."

Delayed-Notice Searches Invite Police Abuses

Donald E. Wilkes Jr.

The USA Patriot Act was passed by Congress after the September 11, 2001, terrorist attacks to give law enforcement enhanced powers to combat terrorism. In the following viewpoint Donald E. Wilkes Jr. argues that delayed-notice searches, authorized by section 213 of the act, allow limitless potential for police abuses. Unlike traditional searches, which suspects know about, these "sneak and peek" searches are conducted without the suspects' knowledge, Wilkes claims. In consequence, he contends, such searches constitute a gross violation of Fourth Amendment rights, which prohibit unfair searches and seizures. A prolific author on legal issues, Wilkes is a professor at the University of Georgia School of Law.

As you read, consider the following questions:

1. As stated by the author, why do sneak and peek warrants generally require breaking and entering suspects' premises?

2. If physical objects are removed from a suspect's home under a sneak and peek warrant, what is one way the police may ensure that the removal remains clandestine, according to Wilkes?

3. What would have to be done to get the sneak and peek provision of the Patriot Act struck off the books, according to Wilkes?

In his recent article "Taking Liberty with Freedom," author Richard P. Moore reminds us that the USA Patriot Act, signed by President [George W.] Bush [on Oct. 26, 2001,] in the wake of the Sept. 11 terrorist attacks, "gives the government the kind of sweeping powers of arrest, detention, surveillance, investigation, deportation, and search and seizure that . . . assault . . . our most basic freedoms."

"No hearings were held in either the House or Senate on the USA Patriot Act," legal scholar John Dean tells us, "and few—if any—members of Congress were really aware of what was actually in this massive, complex, highly technical 30,000-word statute, which is divided into ten titles, with more than 270 sections and endless subsections that cross-reference and amend a dozen or more different laws."

A Monstrous Statute

I want to examine here a single section of the USA Patriot Act—section 213, definitely one of the most sinister provisions of this monstrous statute.

In euphemistic language that conceals the provision's momentous significance, section 213 states that with regard to federal search warrants "any notice required . . . to be given may be delayed if . . . [1] the court finds reasonable cause to believe that providing immediate notification of the execution of the warrant may have an adverse result ... ; [2] the warrant prohibits the seizure of any tangible property ... except where the court finds reasonable necessity for the seizure; and [3] the warrant provides for the giving of such notice within a reasonable period of its execution, which period may thereafter be extended by the court for good cause shown."

Section 213 may be couched in Orwellian terminology, but there is no doubt about what it does.

Section 213 is the first statute ever enacted in the history of American criminal procedure to specifically authorize an entirely new form of search warrant—what legal scholars call the sneak and peek warrant (also dubbed the covert entry warrant or the surreptitious entry warrant). A sneak and peek search warrant authorizes police to effect physical entry into private premises without the owner's or the occupant's permission or knowledge to conduct a search; generally, such entry requires a breaking and entering. In authorizing search warrants to be served stealthily, sneak and peek warrants are a radical departure from conventional search warrants.

Radically Different Searches

Inhabitants of premises searched under a conventional warrant know of the search either at the time it occurs or shortly thereafter. This is because traditionally search warrants have been executed openly and at a time when the inhabitants of the premises searched are present. Conventional search warrants authorize the seizure of physical objects (such as drugs or stolen property); if such articles are found and taken away by police the occupants will certainly know it. (Indeed, if possession of the articles is illegal, the occupants will be arrested on possession charges.) In addition, conventional search warrants require police to give a copy of the warrant and a receipt for any items seized to the persons present on the premises, or else leave the copy and the receipt on the premises. In those

What's Left of Your Privacy

During the covert search [authorized by Section 213 of the Patriot Act], agents can take photographs, seize physical property, examine a computer's hard drive and insert the digital "magic lantern," also known as the "sniffer keystroke logger." Once installed, the program creates a record of every stroke you make, whether you transmit it over the Internet or not. On another unannounced "sneak-and-peek" search, the agents can download that information—which constitutes an additional government invasion of what's left of your privacy.

Nat Hentoff, Washington Times, *August 4, 2003.*
www.washtimes.com.

instances where no one is present when the warrant is served the occupants will nevertheless usually soon be aware of the search and seizure: there will be signs of a forcible entry; the premises will have been ransacked and any seized items will be missing; and a copy of the warrant and the receipt will be on the premises.

The regime of sneak and peek warrants is drastically different. We know this because in the 1980's the FBI [Federal Bureau of Investigation] and the DEA [Drug Enforcement Administration] managed, incredibly, to persuade certain federal judges to issue at least 35 sneak and peek warrants, despite the absence of any statutory authorization for such warrants at the time; and there are five reported federal appellate court decisions detailing the facts concerning the issuance and execution of such warrants.

Under a sneak and peek warrant the search occurs only when the occupants are absent from the premises. The entry, search, and any seizures are conducted in such a way as to keep them secret. The search and seizure focus on obtaining intangibles; i.e., information concerning what has been going on, or now is inside, the premises. Photographs may be taken. Usually, no physical objects are removed. If objects are removed this is accomplished in such a way that the removal remains clandestine; for example, an item seized might be replaced with another item that appears to be the original. No copy of the warrant or receipt is left on the premises. Sometimes the same premises is subjected to repeated covert entries under successive warrants. Generally, it will not be until after the police make an arrest or return with a conventional search warrant that the existence of any covert entries is disclosed. This may be weeks or even months after the surreptitious search or searches.

Warrants Are Not Restricted to Terrorists

Although section 213, like the USA Patriot Act itself, was ostensibly designed to suppress terrorism, the section is not restricted to terrorists or terrorism offenses; it may be used in connection with any federal crime, including misdemeanors. Section 213 also is exempted from the Act's sunset provisions and therefore will remain on the books permanently unless repealed. Although section 213 governs federal search warrants, it is only a question of time before states begin enacting legislation authorizing state and local police to obtain sneak and peek warrants from state judges.

If a sneak and peek warrant targets a person who, as it turns out, is in fact innocent and the search uncovers nothing criminal, it is unlikely that the victim of the search will ever find out about it.

Exactly who, after all, is going to make sure that police notify such a person of the search? At any rate, police will rarely admit that an innocent person was subjected to a covert search, even when it did happen, because police can be counted on, whenever they deem it necessary to protect themselves, to plant evidence or to testify falsely as to what they observed. Where the search is surreptitious and the occupants are not present to observe the search the potential for police abuse is limitless. The widespread problem of lawlessness in law enforcement in this country will simply become exacerbated under a system where police learn at the police academy how to clandestinely burglarize the premises of Americans.

Standard Operating Procedure

It may also be expected that over time the use of sneak and peek warrants will tend to become common rather than exceptional. Search warrants are issued on an ex parte basis; at the time a warrant is issued no one knows that police have requested it, or that a judge has granted the request, except the police and the judge. The judges who issue search warrants are usually low-level magistrates who rubberstamp whatever police request, and police constantly strive to expand their power by using increasingly aggressive investigative techniques.

Furthermore, the history of American criminal procedure conclusively shows that intrusive investigative procedures which police claim they need to use on special occasions to deal with the worst criminals soon become standard operating procedures used against ordinary suspects.

Take, for example, the use of no-knock search warrants in Georgia. These warrants, which permit police to burst into occupied homes unannounced, came into existence because police claimed there were some dangerous criminals who would resist entry or destroy evidence if (as traditionally has been required) police were to announce their purpose and authority before forcibly entering to execute a conventional search warrant. But no-knock search warrants (which, despite their frequent use, are not authorized by statute in [Georgia]) have become the rule instead of the exception in Georgia. Over a decade ago the Georgia Court of Appeals pointed out that such warrants "simply have become customary . . . in drug cases." (The overwhelming majority of all search warrants involve drugs.) . . .

No Check on Agents

Undoubtedly section 213 will be challenged in court on grounds it violates Fourth Amendment protections against unreasonable searches and seizures. However, the federal courts are packed with statists and majoritarians appointed by [presidents] Nixon, Reagan, and both Bushes for the specific purpose of narrowing "the right of criminals" and strengthening "the peace forces." These judges have, with a few exceptions, displayed unremitting hostility to Fourth Amendment rights, handing down decision after decision expanding police investigative powers at the expense of individual privacy. In 1979, in one of the worst Fourth Amendment decisions of all time, the U.S. Supreme Court upheld the validity of covert entries into private premises by federal police to install court-authorized listening devices, even though the federal electronic surveillance statute is starkly silent on the issue of covert entries. Law reviews are now filled with articles with such titles as "The Incredible Shrinking Fourth Amendment" and "The Court That Devoured the Fourth Amendment." There is, therefore, no possibility that the federal courts will hold sneak and peek warrants to violate the Fourth Amendment.

Nearly two decades ago a courageous federal judge, in a dissenting opinion, warned that sneak and peek search warrants "constitute . . . a dangerous and radical threat to civil rights and to the security of all our homes and persons." Echoing this sentiment, an article in the *San Diego Law Review* several years later emphasized that sneak and peek search warrants "bestow on law enforcement agents unlimited license to rifle through a person's private residence without the owner's knowledge or consent. There is no check on agents' actions to ensure they comply" with protections for individual rights, and "the risk of abuse and the subsequent intrusion into privacy is . . . severe."

Until Congress repeals it, section 213 means that from now on Americans will, in the words of another law review article, published in the *Stanford Law Review,* be forced to live in "Orwellian fear that government agents may intrude secretly at any time."

> *"Section 213 [of the Patriot Act, authorizing delayed-notice searches] is a reasonable statutory codification of a long-standing law-enforcement tool that enables us to better protect the public from terrorists."*

Delayed-Notice Searches Are Needed to Thwart Terrorism

Chuck Rosenberg

In the following viewpoint, originally given as testimony before a congressional subcommittee on May 3, 2005, Chuck Rosenberg defends the effectiveness and constitutionality of delayed-notice search warrants. According to Rosenberg, although the Patriot Act simplified the rules governing such searches—which allow law enforcement agents to delay notifying the subject of a search—delayed-notice searches have been conducted for years. Moreover, he claims, these searches have been deemed constitutional by the courts. Rosenberg contends that delayed-notice searches are necessary to conduct successful investigations into terrorist activities. An attorney, Rosenberg has held several positions in the U.S. Department of Justice. In June 2005 he was appointed U.S. attorney for the southern district of Texas.

Chuck Rosenberg, excerpted from testimony before the United States House of Representatives Subcommittee on Crime, Terrorism and Homeland Security, Committee on the Judiciary, May 3, 2005.

As you read, consider the following questions:

1. Who has the authority to issue delayed-notice search warrants, according to Rosenberg?
2. As stated by the author, who determines how long law-enforcement officers can wait before notifying a suspect that a search and/or seizure has been carried out?
3. The U.S. Department of Justice estimates that it uses delayed-notice warrants in what percentage of all warrants issued, according to Rosenberg?

It is my pleasure to appear before [the U.S. House of Representatives] to discuss section 213 of the USA PATRIOT Act, relating to delayed-notice search warrants. This provision has been an invaluable tool in our efforts to prevent terrorism and combat crime.

In passing the USA PATRIOT Act, Congress recognized that delayed-notice search warrants are a vital aspect of the Department [of Justice's] strategy of prevention: detecting and incapacitating terrorists, drug dealers and other criminals before they can harm our nation. Delayed-notice search warrants are a long-standing, crime-fighting tool upheld as constitutional by courts nationwide for decades. Such warrants were not created by the USA PATRIOT Act and had been regularly used prior to 2001 in investigations involving drugs, child pornography, and other criminal offenses. Section 213 simply established explicit statutory authority for investigators and prosecutors to ask a federal judge for permission to delay temporarily notice that a search warrant was executed. This statutory authority created a uniform standard for the issuance of these warrants, thus ensuring that delayed-notice search warrants are evaluated under the same criteria across the nation.

Notice Still Required

As with any other search warrant, a delayed-notice search warrant is issued by a federal judge only upon a showing that there is probable cause to believe that the property to be searched or items to be seized constitute evidence of a criminal offense. A delayed-notice warrant differs from an ordinary search warrant only in that the judge specifically authorizes that the law-enforcement officers executing the warrant may wait for a court-authorized period of time before notifying the subject of the search that a search was executed. To be clear, section 213 still requires law enforcement to give notice in all cases that property has been searched or seized. It only allows for a delay in notice for a reasonable period of time—a time period defined by a federal judge under certain clear and narrow circumstances.

Federal courts have consistently ruled that delayed-notice search warrants are constitutional and do not violate the Fourth Amendment. In *Dalia v. United States*, for example, the U.S. Supreme Court held that the Fourth Amendment does not require law enforcement to give immediate notice of the execution of a search warrant. Since *Dalia*, three federal courts of appeals have considered the constitutionality of delayed-notice search warrants, and all three have upheld their constitutionality.

To my knowledge, no court has ever held otherwise. Long before the enactment of the USA PATRIOT Act, it was clear that delayed notification was appropriate in certain circumstances; that remains true today. Section 213 of the USA PATRIOT Act simply resolved the mix of inconsistent rules, practices and court decisions varying from circuit to circuit, by mandating uniform and equitable application of this authority across the nation.

Reasonable Cause

Under section 213, investigators and prosecutors seeking a judge's approval to delay notification must show that, if made contemporaneous to the search, there is reasonable cause to believe that notification might:

1. Endanger the life or physical safety of an individual;
2. Cause flight from prosecution;
3. Result in destruction of, or tampering with, evidence;
4. Result in intimidation of potential witnesses; or
5. Cause serious jeopardy to an investigation or unduly delay a trial.

It is only in these five narrow circumstances that the department may request judicial approval to delay notification, and a federal judge must agree with the department's evaluation before approving any delay.

Delayed-notice search warrants provide a crucial option to law enforcement. If immediate notification were required regardless of the circumstances, law-enforcement officials often would be forced to make a difficult choice: delay the urgent need to conduct a search or conduct the search and prematurely notify the target of the existence of law-enforcement interest in his or her illegal conduct and undermine the equally pressing need to keep the ongoing investigation confidential.

Jeopardizing an Investigation

It appears as though there is widespread agreement that delayed-notice search warrants should be available in four of the five circumstances listed above. If immediate notice would endanger the life or physical safety of an individual, cause flight from prosecution, result in the destruction of evidence, or lead to witness intimidation, a general consensus exists that it is reasonable and appropriate to delay temporarily notice that a search has been conducted. However, the remaining circumstance—serious jeopardy to an investigation—has been the source of some controversy and I therefore wish to discuss it in more detail.

If a federal judge concludes that immediate notice of a search might seriously jeopardize an ongoing investigation, the Department of Justice strongly believes that it is entirely

Tying Officers' Hands

The loss of Section 213 [of the USA-PATRIOT Act] would result in less vigorous investigations, more terrorism, more crime, less safety for our citizens, and possibly injury or death to individuals ranging from witnesses in investigations to the innocent victims of terrorism.

This issue is that important.

We can defeat terrorism without giving up our liberties. We can defeat terrorism without stepping outside the bounds of the Constitution. However, we cannot defeat terrorists by tying the hands of law enforcement.

Thomas E. Johnston, West Virginia State Journal, *June 2, 2005.*

appropriate that the provision of such notice be delayed temporarily. There are a variety of ways in which immediate notice might seriously jeopardize an investigation, and investigators and prosecutors should not be precluded from obtaining a delayed-notice search warrant simply because their request does not fall into one of the other four circumstances listed in the statute.

A prime example of the importance of this provision occurred when the Justice Department obtained a delayed-notice search warrant for a Federal Express package that contained counterfeit credit cards. At the time of the search, it was important not to disclose the existence of this federal investigation, as this would have exposed a related wiretap that was targeting major drug trafficking activities.

A multi-agency task force was engaged in a lengthy investigation that culminated in the indictment of the largest drug-trafficking organization ever prosecuted in the Western District of Pennsylvania. A total of 51 defendants were indicted on drug, money laundering and firearms charges, and its leaders received very lengthy sentences of imprisonment.

This organization was responsible for bringing thousands of kilograms of cocaine and heroin into Western Pennsylvania. Cooperation was obtained from selected defendants and their cooperation was used to obtain indictments against individuals in New York who supplied the heroin and cocaine. Thousands of dollars in real estate, automobiles, jewelry and cash were forfeited.

This case had a discernible and positive impact upon the North Side of Pittsburgh, where the organization was based. The DEA [Drug Enforcement Administration] reported that the availability of heroin and cocaine in this region decreased as a result of the successful elimination of this major drug trafficking organization.

While the drug investigation was ongoing, it became clear that several of the conspirators had ties to an ongoing credit card fraud operation. An investigation into the credit card fraud led to the search of a Fed Ex package that contained fraudulent credit cards. Had notice of this search been given at the time of the search, however, the drug investigation would have been seriously jeopardized because an existing . . . wiretap would have been endangered. This is just one ordinary example of this extraordinarily important tool.

A Reasonable, Long-Standing Tool

The use of a delayed-notice search warrant is the exception, not the rule. In total, the government has sought delayed-notification search warrants approximately 155 times under section 213 of the USA PATRIOT Act.

Law enforcement agents and investigators provide immediate notice of a search warrant's execution in the vast majority of cases. According to the Administrative Office of the U.S. Courts (AOUSC), during a 12-month period ending September 30, 2003, U.S. District Courts handled 32,539 search warrants. By contrast, in one 14-month period between April 2003 and July 2004 the department used the section 213 authority approximately 60 times according to a department survey. The department therefore estimates that it seeks to delay notice with respect to less than 0.2% of all search warrants issued.

[In April 2005], the department supplemented earlier information made public regarding the use of section 213 by releasing information derived from a survey of all United States Attorneys' offices covering the period between April 1, 2003, and January 31, 2005. Nationwide, section 213 was used approximately 108 times over that 22-month period. Of those 108 times, the authority was exercised in less than half of the federal judicial districts across the country. Furthermore, the department has asked the courts to find reasonable necessity for seizure in connection with a delayed-notification search warrant approximately 45 times. In every case where the Justice Department sought a delayed-notification search warrant during that period, a court has approved. It is possible to misconstrue this information as evidence that courts merely "rubber stamp" the department's requests. In reality, however, it is an indication that the department takes the authority codified by the USA PATRIOT Act very seriously. We seek court approval only in those rare circumstances—those that fit the narrowly tailored statute—when it is absolutely necessary and justified.

In sum, delayed-notice search warrants have been used for decades by law enforcement, but are used only infrequently and scrupulously—in appropriate situations where we can demonstrate reasonable cause to believe that immediate notice would harm individuals or compromise investigations, and even then only with a judge's express approval. Section 213 is a reasonable statutory codification of a long-standing law-enforcement tool that enables us to better protect the public from terrorists and criminals while preserving Americans' constitutional rights.

"If al-Qaeda has created an atmosphere in which an ordinary person can have five bullets pumped into him by the police, and society shrugs its shoulders, then the terrorists have already won a modest victory."

Police Shoot-to-Kill Policies Invite Abuse of Force

Tim Hames

On July 22, 2005—the day after the second spate of terrorist bombings in London, England, in a two-week period—the London Metropolitan Police shot dead an innocent man they suspected to be a suicide bomber. In the following viewpoint Tim Hames acknowledges the difficulty police officers face when confronted with a suspect they believe may be ready to detonate a deadly bomb. Yet he still decries the shoot-to-kill policy that led to the innocent man's death, and he criticizes what he sees as widespread indifference to the incident. Hames has written widely on politics in both the United States and the United Kingdom. He is an assistant editor, chief editorial writer, and columnist for the Times, *a London newspaper.*

Tim Hames, "Oops, Sorry, Won't Do. We Can't Just Shrug Our Shoulders Over This Shooting," The *Times*, London, July 25, 2005. Copyright © 2005 Times Newspapers Ltd. Reproduced by permission.

As you read, consider the following questions:

1. How did the leader of Liberty, a British human-rights organization, react to the police shooting in London on July 22, 2005, according to Hames?
2. According to the author, how did the police react after the shooting?
3. What three consequences does Hames recommend should take place as a result of the police shooting?

The police, according to a Sunday newspaper [on July 24, 2005], fear a "backlash in the Muslim community" after the fatal shooting of Jean Charles de Menezes, an innocent Brazilian electrician, at Stockwell Tube [subway] station on Friday [July 22, 2005]. What the police should fear is a backlash from the entire civilised community. Yet there is no evidence that either the politicians or the public will provide it. The theme has been that this was a tragic "mistake", but one which was unavoidable, even inevitable, in the current climate.

The breadth of the coalition of "Oh dear, but . . ." in this instance is astonishing. Ken Livingstone, the Mayor of London, who can normally be relied on for controversy, has declined to condemn either the specifics of this event or the shoot-to-kill strategy behind it. The Liberal Democrats, whose purpose in life, surely, is to defend civil rights in difficult times, are similarly reticent. Muslim Labour MPs [members of Parliament], such as Khalid Mahmood have urged caution. Even Shami Chakrabarti, the director of Liberty [a British human-rights organization], has given warning against a "rush to judgment". It has been left to the Brazilian Government to express anger about the manner in which Mr Menezes died.

Police Inconsistency

It should not be angry alone. I am a hardliner on the War on Terror and remain a hawk on the invasion of Iraq and its af-

Better to Have Living Suspects than Corpses

The [London] police are now sorry they accidentally killed an innocent they suspected of being a suicide bomber, but I can certainly understand the mistake. In the end, the best solution is to train police officers and then leave the decision to them. But honestly, policies that are more likely to result in living incarcerated suspects . . . that can be interrogated are better than policies that are more likely to result in corpses.

Bruce Schneier, "Schneier on Security," July 25, 2005.
www.schneier.com.

termath. But if al-Qaeda has created an atmosphere in which an ordinary person can have five bullets pumped into him by the police, and society shrugs its shoulders, then the terrorists have already won a modest victory.

The inconsistency bordering on callousness of Scotland Yard [the headquarters of the Greater London Metropolitan Police] has been breathtaking. It was initially suggested that Mr Menezes was under surveillance and had been approached after he walked from his residence in Stockwell to the Tube station. It is now clear that he started his trip from Tulse Hill, where he had stayed at someone else's home, was watched, was noted wearing bulky clothing, yet was allowed (despite the slaughter [on a London bus] at Tavistock Square on July 7 and the attempted blast on a double-decker [bus] at Hackney [on July 21, 2005,]) to board a bus for a 15-minute journey and was challenged only when he sought to buy an Underground [subway] ticket. Why was someone whom the police continue to insist was a "potential suicide-bomber" no menace on the No 2 bus, but an urgent threat who had to be taken out when moving in the direction of the Northern [subway] Line?

And then there was the attempt to "spin" this situation to suit the police immediately after the shooting. It must have been obvious within minutes that the man concerned had no explosives on him and it is highly likely that he had identifying documentation. Yet for hours on Friday police sources were briefing that this shooting was "directly connected" to their inquiries into the botched bombings of July 21 [2005] and over the weekend the implication rumbled on that he had lived in, or perhaps near, or somewhere quite close to, multi-occupancy accommodation that had been deemed "suspicious".

Blaming the Victim

This attempt to blame Mr Menezes for his own death continues unabated. It was hinted that he might have been an illegal immigrant, as if that justifies what occurred. It has been argued that it was "irresponsible" of him to wear a quilted jacket in July, as if that were a crime. There are, furthermore, "no excuses", it is intoned, for the fact that he ran when armed plainclothes police officers shouted at him.

I don't know about you, but if I found myself minding my own business on the São Paulo metro [in Brazil] and was suddenly confronted by men wearing no uniforms but wielding weapons, screaming at me in Portuguese, I too might choose to bolt for it. It was not merely the police but their victim who had to make a split-second decision.

At a minimum, the Metropolitan Police should be expressing something a little stronger than "regret" and admitting unambiguous, if partially understandable, responsibility for this outrage. Yet the spirit in which they are operating was summed up by Lord Stevens, the former Commissioner of the Met, in his *News of the World* column. . . . Now Sir John

Stevens, as he was, was an admirable public servant and he does make a number of compelling points about the pressure that the police are under and the unique dangers posed by suicide bombers. Even so, to dismiss this death as an "error" that should not result in the shoot-to-kill policy being reviewed verges on the sadistic. "My heart goes out," Lord Stevens wrote, not to the Menezes family, but to "the officer who killed the man in Stockwell Tube Station." Well, up to a point, Lord Copper.

Re-examine 'Shoot-to-Kill' Policy

There should be three consequences of this terrible tragedy. The first is that every aspect of the investigation that will be conducted by the Independent Police Complaints Commission should be published. There must not be the slightest possibility that the Metropolitan Police might be covering up its embarrassment by, for example, citing "operational reasons" why the decisions taken . . . cannot be scrutinised. The second is that the shoot-to-kill policy has to be re-examined. There is a world of difference between a plainclothes policeman finding himself riding on the Tube and spotting a man with a large bag behaving in a manner that makes him a potential suicide bomber and shooting him, and chasing a person on to a train carriage and firing at him.

The final and most important aspect relates to Mr Menezes and his loved ones. This man was, in effect, as much a victim of the London bombs of July 7 as those who died then. It is inconceivable that he would have been killed by the police if those terrorist atrocities had not happened. His name should be included among those who will be supported by the fund that was set up to help those left behind after those murders. We must be honest about how his awful death took place and be ready to learn the lessons.

> *"Introducing restrictions on our free-doms and giving broader—and at times deadlier—discretion to our security forces might be the price democracies must pay for their own defense."*

Police Shoot-to-Kill Policies Are Necessary to Stop Suicide Bombers

Emanuele Ottolenghi

Emanuele Ottolenghi argues in the following viewpoint that shoot-to-kill policies are justified in order to protect citizens against terrorists. He laments the shooting of suspected terrorist Jean Charles de Menezes by London police officers in July 2005, but he claims the officers had little choice but to kill him. Better to shoot a potential suicide bomber than risk the suspect detonating a device that could kill hundreds, the author maintains. He argues that civil liberties must be restricted in times of national crisis. Ottolenghi teaches Israel studies at the Middle East Center of St. Antony's College, Oxford University, in England.

Emanuele Ottolenghi, "Life and Liberty: Democracy at War," *National Review*, July 29, 2005. Copyright © 2005 by National Review, Inc., 215 Lexington Avenue, New York, NY 10016. Reproduced by permission.

As you read, consider the following questions:

1. How do Europeans think terrorism ought to be fought, in Ottolenghi's opinion?
2. According to Ottolenghi, under what two conditions do democracies limit their various freedoms?
3. What is terrorism's ultimate target, in the author's view?

T he death of Jean Charles de Menezes . . . is a tragedy.

One day after the second spate of terror attacks hit London [in July 2005] and with four terrorists still at large, Menezes was mistaken by the [London] metropolitan police as a terrorist and, upon failing to obey orders to halt he was shot five times at close range as he entered a crowded train at a metro station. Bad policing maybe, but what if he had been the right guy? What if he was a terrorist and was about to detonate an explosive belt to kill scores of innocent bystanders? No tears would be shed and those policemen who shot him would be heroes now. The difference between a successful counterterrorism operation and a tragic blunder was, in the final analysis, predicated upon bad intelligence and a split-second decision, something that the war on terrorism will continue to experience. And the context and circumstances of the event suggest that the police acted reasonably. Still, an innocent man is dead and with terrorists still at large democracies owe themselves a moment of reflection. What price must democracy pay to defeat terrorism?

Fighting War

Americans have apparently understood the nature of the terrorist threat. They know they are at war. Despite bombings in London and Madrid and the murder of Dutch filmmaker Theo Van Gogh, Europe seems to believe terrorism can be fought with the same means used for ordinary crime. But fighting crime and fighting a war are two different businesses ndeed. That is why when Menezes was killed in broad daylight by plainclothes policemen in the midst of a terrified crowd many disapproved even before they knew he was innocent. Even if he had been a terrorist, arrest would have been preferable.

As in the case of Israel's policy of targeted killings, even those who understand the plight of the Jewish state often demand that terrorists be apprehended and brought to justice, decrying the action as "extra-judicial killings." Better a terrorist apprehended alive of course, for a host of reasons. Is this feasible though, especially in the age of suicide bombers, or is this enunciation of principle just a recipe for inaction?

One can sympathize with the opinion that no freedom should be sacrificed on the altar of security, but unless this is qualified, in the [time after the September 11, 2001, terrorist attacks] this view is neither serious nor realistic.

Suspended Freedoms

It is not serious, because liberalism has always postulated the possibility of a temporary suspension of freedoms to confront national emergencies. States of emergencies are regulated in liberal democracies so as not to allow disproportionate measures: the extent of restrictions must be correlated to the nature of the threat. In war and catastrophe, democracies accept limits on freedom of the press, movement, immigration, expression and assembly, rationing and curfews, military courts and anti-sedition laws.

It is not realistic, because terrorism exploits the openness of free societies to pursue its deadly designs. Our strength—a robust civil society that keeps [a tyrannical government] at permanent arm's length—has become our weakness when confronted with terrorists in our midst. Tolerant immigration laws, due process, and a host of mechanisms expressing confidence in the freedom we cherish and the desire of all human beings to enjoy its gift have made it easier for terrorists, who

Shooting Demonstrates Police Courage

[The police shooting in London of an innocent man on July 22, 2005, was a] demonstration of the courage and professionalism of the police force. In the most dangerous of contexts, a man draws suspicion upon himself. Refusing to stop, he hares off into the Underground. The police pursue him, although they could be running towards their own deaths. They catch him and dispatch him in the manner designed to minimise the risk of his being able to explode a bomb.

If Mr [Jean Charles] de Menezes had been a terrorist, the policeman who shot him would now be in line for a gallantry medal.

Bruce Anderson, London Independent, *July 2005.*
http://comment.independent.co.uk.

loathe freedom and exalt death, to strike. Introducing restrictions on our freedoms and giving broader—and at times deadlier—discretion to our security forces might be the price democracies must pay for their own defense.

Dilemmas and Challenges

Nevertheless, liberals have a point: If the knee-jerk reaction that postulates no limits is silly, this does not mean that anything goes. The shoot-to-kill policy tragically applied [on July 22, 2005,] in London was meant to save innocent lives: a balance had to be struck between a suspected terrorist and his right to life and the right to life of innocent bystanders. But that balance is frail and fraught with moral dilemmas, as the death of Menezes proves. This tragic outcome highlighted both the dilemmas and the challenges a democracy must face if it wants to defeat terrorism and still be true to its moral higher grounds.

Still, in real-life situations, the ideal may prove impossible to achieve.

To maintain the same level of individual freedoms under the new threat of terrorism might therefore prove to be a principled but untenable stance, which one can hope to hold only at the price of giving in to terror's blackmail. But make no mistake: Ultimately, terror's goal is not just to influence a change in policy among Western societies, as many in Europe claim. Terror's ultimate target is the Western way of life itself, which is built on freedom. Old principles will not work this time. To save freedom and fight terror at the same time a new doctrine is needed. To what extent are Western societies prepared to limit civil liberties in order to effectively countenance the terrorist threat? The answer cannot be a dogmatic refusal to ponder the dilemma. The only right answer is to find a balance between the call of liberty and the imperative of security. To engage this debate, rather than shun it, is the only way to ensure that freedom is protected in the long term.

Governments' primary duty is to protect their citizens from outside (and internal) enemies. If there can be no pursuit of happiness without liberty, there is no liberty (or liberty would be meaningless), surely, unless life is first protected.

Periodical Bibliography

The following articles have been selected to supplement the diverse views presented in this chapter.

Bruce Ackerman "The Perils of Judicial Restraint: If the Supreme Court Won't Intervene on 'Enemy Combatant' Cases, Congress Must," *Slate*, April 5, 2006.

America "The Patriot Act and Civil Liberties," August 1, 2005.

John Barry, Michael Hirsh, and Michael Isikoff "The Roots of Torture," *Newsweek*, May 24, 2004.

Bruce W. Burton "The 'O.K. Corral Principle' in the Age of Terrorism: Proposed New Protocols for Judicial Notice in Cases of Alleged Misconduct by Law Enforcement," *Idaho Law Review*, vol. 41, no. 1, Fall 2004.

Anthony Lewis "One Liberty at a Time," *Mother Jones*, May/June 2004.

Jason Miller "Democratizing the World: One Torture Victim at a Time," Countercurrents.org, March 24, 2006. www.countercurrents.org.

Edward T. Pound and Linda Robinson "A Place Dante Might Like," *U.S. News & World Report*, May 31, 2004.

Harvey Silverglate "Civil Liberties and Enemy Combatants: Why the Supreme Court's Widely Praised Rulings Are Bad for America," *Reason*, January 1, 2005.

Ann Scott Tyson "Lessons from Abu Ghraib," *Christian Science Monitor*, May 5, 2004.

OPPOSING
VIEWPOINTS®
SERIES

CHAPTER 4

How Can Police Misconduct Be Reduced?

Chapter Preface

Some people believe that only the threat of prison time for officers convicted in excessive force cases will reduce the incidence of police brutality. Critics of this approach note that even when officers are brought to trial, juries often acquit, and when they don't, appeals courts frequently overturn convictions. Can court rulings be counted on to help reduce police misconduct?

As the interpreter of federal laws and the U.S. Constitution, the U.S. Supreme Court sets the standard for lower-court decisions in matters of civil liberties versus law enforcement power. A notable example is the *Miranda v. Arizona* decision of 1966, which requires arresting officers to immediately inform suspects of their legal protection against self-incrimination and their right to legal representation; without this step, any resulting confession is supposed to be inadmissible in court.

As the Court moved steadily toward the political right under the leadership of William H. Rehnquist, who was the chief justice from 1986 until his death in 2005, however, new rulings incrementally narrowed the application of decisions such as *Miranda* without fully overturning them. Since these cases generally deal with obscure points of constitutional law, they typically escape the headlines garnered by landmark cases. Yet, it is the lesser-known decisions that, in a cumulative fashion, shape the culture in which issues such as police brutality are addressed in the legal system.

Virtually every American is familiar with the Supreme Court's *Bush v. Gore* ruling that decided the outcome of the presidential election of 2000. By contrast, the 2001 *Saucier v. Katz* decision went virtually unnoticed. This case upheld and strengthened the principle of "qualified immunity" for police officers accused of using excessive force and added a new layer of legal fact-finding to the process of filing brutality charges against a police officer. The result is that fewer cases will land in court in the first place.

In 2005, John G. Roberts replaced Rehnquist as chief justice, and in 2006, Samuel A. Alito replaced retiring associate justice Sandra Day O'Connor. While no one can predict how these two conservative justices will rule on any specific matter, their past arguments suggest that the Supreme Court will not soon break any new ground in protecting individuals from police officers accused of using excessive force.

According to the Alliance for Justice, Roberts holds a "narrow view of the vital role our courts and our government play in safeguarding individual rights. . . . By contrast, he holds an expansive view of presidential power and law enforcement authority." Regarding Alito, the Alliance for Justice notes that on two occasions as a lower-court judge, Alito voted "to uphold intrusive police searches of women and children who were not named in search warrants and were not the subjects of any investigation."

While the threat of legal accountability may not provide a strong deterrent to police misconduct in the future, activists are hopeful that other approaches will be effective. The authors in this chapter weigh the strengths and weaknesses of various efforts to control and reduce police misconduct and brutality.

> "The unbridled use of racial profiling
> ... could significantly undermine the
> unfulfilled national commitment to
> making citizens of all races equal un-
> der the law."

Racial Profiling Should Be Eliminated

Nelson Lund

Law-enforcement officers use racial profiling to target people on the basis of their race. Nelson Lund argues in the following viewpoint that the U.S. government has inappropriately loosened its standards on the use of racial profiling in its zeal to combat terrorism. While federal laws forbid the use of profiling while conducting regular police business, they allow its use when law-enforcement officers are investigating terrorist activity. Lund believes that the police will soon claim that all their activities relate to terrorism and will use racial profiling indiscriminately, thereby infringing on Americans' civil liberties. Lund is a professor of law at George Mason University.

Nelson Lund, "The Future of Racial Profiling in the War on Terror," *The CIP Report*, vol. 2, August 2003, p. 7. Reproduced by permission.

As you read, consider the following questions:

1. According to the author, in what exception are federal agencies allowed to consider race in traditional law-enforcement activities?

2. What are the two examples of forbidden behavior offered by the Justice Department in regard to racial profiling in law enforcement, according to Lund?

3. What does Lund cite as the leading case in federal courts regarding racial profiling or stereotyping?

Before [the September 11, 2001, terrorist attacks] we had what looked like a clear national consensus against racial profiling in law enforcement. Although the issue had become controversial, the disputes were almost entirely concerned with whether the police were in fact commonly using forbidden racial stereotypes, especially when choosing which motorists to pull over for traffic violations that are so common that officers necessarily ignore them most of the time. Then came the terrorist attacks. All of the hijackers who carried out the hijackings were Middle Eastern men, and commentators began arguing that racial profiling is an appropriate tool in the war on terrorism. Judge Robert Bork, for example, has neatly distinguished ordinary law enforcement from the new threat we face: "The stigma attached to profiling where it hardly exists has perversely carried over to an area where it should exist but does not: the war against terrorism."

The public seems to agree. Polls have showed strong majorities in favor of subjecting those of Arab descent to extra scrutiny at airports. Interestingly, blacks and Arab-Americans were even more likely than whites to favor such policies. The Bush Administration at first resisted the pressure to employ racial profiling. The Department of Justice, however, has now reversed course and adopted Judge Bork's distinction between ordinary police work and anti-terrorism activities. In June [2003], the Department's Civil Rights Division promulgated a new directive entitled "Guidance Regarding the Use of Race by Federal Law Enforcement Agencies." This document adopts two standards, one for "traditional law enforcement activities," and a very different one for certain other police activities.

A Different Standard

The first standard is faithful to President Bush's pre-9/11 statement that racial profiling is "wrong and we will end it in America." Federal agencies are forbidden to consider race in any "traditional" law enforcement decision, except where officials have trustworthy information linking someone of a specific race to a specific crime, as for example where a credible eyewitness has described a fleeing felon as a member of a particular race, or where a criminal organization is known to comprise members who are overwhelmingly of a given race. Because these exceptions do not entail racial profiling or stereotyping, the Justice Department has effectively imposed a total ban on that practice in traditional law enforcement activities.

A completely different standard is now applicable to federal activities involving threats to "national security or other catastrophic events (including the performance of duties related to air transportation security) or in enforcing laws protecting the integrity of the Nation's borders."

According to the new Justice Department guidance, racial profiling may be used in these contexts whenever it is permitted by the Constitution. This is very close to giving federal officials *carte blanche* to select targets for investigation or especially intensive attention on the basis of racial stereotypes. The applicable constitutional test is called "strict scrutiny." As the Justice Department acknowledges, applying this test is "a fact-intensive process." That is just another way of saying that there is no clearly defined constitutional line between permissible and impermissible uses of racial profiling. And because the Justice Department makes no effort to draw a line be-

Mike Thompson. Reproduced by permission.

tween what it regards as permissible and impermissible, security officials are effectively encouraged to err in the direction of using racial stereotypes whenever they might seem useful.

The only examples of forbidden behavior offered by the Justice Department are two very extreme cases. First, the Department rules out using racial criteria "as a mere pretext for invidious discrimination." This is something that nobody would ever admit to doing. Second, the Department says that a screener may not pick someone out for heightened scrutiny at a checkpoint "solely" because of his race "[i]n the absence of any threat warning."

Continuing Threat Warning

This situation cannot even arise, given that the whole nation is under a constant and continuing "threat warning" that is likely to remain in place for the foreseeable future; thus, the principal implication here is that screeners may indeed focus on individuals "solely" because of their race so long as any threat warning remains in place.

Racial Profiling Does Exist

Although some observers claim that racial profiling doesn't exist, there is an abundance of stories and statistics that document the practice. One case where law enforcement officers were particularly bold in their declaration of intent involved U.S. Forest Service officers in California's Mendocino National Forest. . . . In an attempt to stop marijuana growing, forest rangers were told to question all Hispanics whose cars were stopped, regardless of whether pot was actually found in their vehicles.

Gene Callahan and William Anderson,
"The Roots of Racial Profiling." Reason.com, August 2001.
http://reason.com.

In addition to being inherently "fact intensive," the constitutional test will almost certainly be applied by the courts in a way that is extremely deferential to the discretionary judgments of federal officials. The leading case, *Korematsu v. United States*, upheld the mass internment of Japanese-Americans during World War II, even though the internment program was based entirely on a generalized and unsubstantiated mistrust of Japanese-Americans. Although this decision has frequently been criticized, it has not been overruled. Similarly, the Supreme Court has held that law enforcement decisions based on racial stereotypes do not violate the Fourth Amendment. And, in its most recent decision on racial discrimination, the Court gave extreme deference to the discretionary judgments of government officials who used a form of racial profiling in admissions decisions to a state law school.

Because the government interests at stake in this affirmative action case were clearly much less urgent than those involved in preventing terrorist attacks, one must infer that the

Court has implicitly dictated a virtual hands-off policy with respect to judicial supervision of racial profiling in this context.

Imperfections

The Justice Department's guidance document, which encourages federal agencies involved in anti-terrorism and related activities to employ racial profiling to the full extent permitted by the Constitution, has several serious imperfections, including the following:

First, law enforcement officials now have an incentive to bring ordinary law enforcement activities under the rubric of "national security or other catastrophic events" in order to escape the very strict rules imposed by the Department for traditional law enforcement. If an agent at the DEA [Drug Enforcement Administration] decides that the escape of a particular drug trafficker would be "catastrophic," the Justice Department's guidance does not clearly prohibit him from using racial stereotypes in his investigation. The same goes for many other activities that Congress has thought so threatening that they deserve to be made federal crimes.

Whether or not this bleeding of the categories occurs on a significant scale, the unbridled use of racial profiling as a tool in the war on terrorism and other "catastrophic events" could significantly undermine the unfulfilled national commitment to making citizens of all races equal under the law. Few events could have been more catastrophic than losing World War II, yet almost everyone now recognizes that massive racial profiling, albeit lawful, was a completely inappropriate and unnecessary means of preventing that catastrophe.

No Controls

Finally, the Justice Department has neglected one of the most obvious and well-known pathologies of government bureaucracies. The new policy imposes virtually no controls on the use of racial stereotypes in an indeterminately large class of activities. This will encourage government officials to employ racial stereotypes, and it may foster the lazy use of such stereotypes. The actual effect could well be to impede the war on terrorism. We have a recent example of this danger: the investigation (in which the Department of Justice participated) of the terroristic sniper attacks in the Washington, D.C. area in late 2002. Apparently relying on well-publicized "criminal profiles," according to which random snipers are almost always white males, the police focused their attention on suspects fitting this stereotype. Duly shocked to find that the investigation had been based on a false premise, the Washington police chief memorably remarked: "We were looking for a white van with white people, and we ended up with a blue car with black people." Not the least of the shortcomings in the Justice Department's new policy guidance is that it makes no effort at all to erect safeguards against repetitions of this sort of dysfunctional bureaucratic behavior.

> *"If criminal activity is not evenly distributed across the population, investigatory stops and searches will fall heaviest on individuals who are members of groups who commit most of the crime."*

Racial Profiling Does Not Contribute to Police Misconduct

Heather Mac Donald

In the following viewpoint Heather Mac Donald asserts that racial profiling is justified because the police have to go where crime is. She argues that police do stop and search a disproportionate number of blacks and Latinos, but they do so because these groups commit more crimes than do whites. Mac Donald maintains that racial profiling is an important law-enforcement tool. Mac Donald is a fellow at the Manhattan Institute, a social-policy organization that works to foster greater economic choice and individual responsibility. She is a well-known media commentator and writer on homeland security and policing issues.

Heather Mac Donald, "What Looks Like Profiling Might Just Be Good Policing," *Los Angeles Times*, January 19, 2003. Reproduced by permission of the author.

As you read, consider the following questions:

1. What are three of the behavioral and contextual clues that Mac Donald says may prompt police officers to search a suspect?

2. According to the author, how do crime rates in Los Angeles reflect the city's ethnic diversity?

3. What is the most frequent complaint about policing from residents of high-crime areas, as reported by Mac Donald?

Los Angeles' perennial critics of the cops are going to have to decide: Do they want policing that mirrors the demographics of the city or goes after criminals? They cannot have it both ways.

Recently released data compiled by the Los Angeles Police Department as part of a federal consent decree show that the city's officers are more likely to ask black and Latino drivers to step out of their cars after stopping them than their white counterparts. Once out of their cars, members of these minorities are more likely to be patted down or searched. Ipso facto, say the critics, L.A. cops discriminate against minorities.

Crime Drives Police Actions

Not so fast. To the charge that the police have "too many" law enforcement interactions with minorities, the question must always be: "Too many" compared to what? To compare stop, search and arrest data to demographics, as cop critics would have us do, is absurd. The police don't formulate their crime strategies based on census findings; they go where the crime is.

What's more, an officer's decision to ask a person to step out of a car or to search that person is triggered by behavioral and contextual cues—nervousness, threatening behavior, resemblance to a suspect, absence of a license and car registration, tinted windows, among others—that are not even remotely captured by demographics.

To benchmark police activity, one must start, at a bare minimum, with the rate of lawbreaking among various groups, for it is ultimately criminal behavior and its consequences that drive police actions. Any disparities in crime rates will have compounding effects throughout the law enforcement system.

For example, [in 2002] a man with a gold tooth was robbing and viciously beating up pedestrians in Mid-City. Victims identified him as either a dark-skinned Latino or a light-skinned African American. Accordingly, if an officer made a traffic stop in the area and noticed that the driver had a gold tooth and was black or Latino, the driver probably would have been asked to step out of his car, frisked and possibly even taken to the station house for a line-up. Some 15 men were stopped before a bike officer caught the actual criminal jaywalking.

Crime Rates Are Lopsided

Those 15 brief detentions went into the LAPD database, but the racial disparities they suggest are misleading. If criminal activity is not evenly distributed across the population, investigatory stops and searches will fall heaviest on individuals who are members of groups who commit most of the crime.

In Los Angeles, crime rates are in fact lopsided. In 2001, blacks committed 41% of all robberies, according to victims' descriptions given to the LAPD, though they constitute only 11% of the city's population. Robbery victims named whites, who make up 30% of the population, 4% of the time, while Latinos, 46% of the population, were identified as the assailant in 45% of such crimes. The figures for aggravated assault and rape are similarly skewed. Only if the police searching for the gold-toothed robber had arbitrarily stopped some whites could they have avoided contributing to racially disproportionate data.

The Supreme Court's Two-Part Test

The Constitution guarantees all persons, including non-citizens, due process and equal protection of the laws. Yet those rights are not absolute. The Supreme Court has insisted that the government pass a rigorous two-part test if it intends to discriminate on the basis of race or national origin. First, government must show that it has a "compelling interest" in employing its discriminatory scheme. Surely, protection against the kind of terror that we experienced on September 11, [2001,] would qualify as compelling. But second, government may not discriminate unless it adopts means that are "least restrictive" when compared against alternative approaches to accomplish the same ends. That second principle will ultimately control disputes over ethnic profiling.

Robert A. Levy, "Ethnic Profiling:
A Rational and Moral Framework," CATO Institute,
October 2, 2001. www.cato.org.

Multiply this problem tens of thousands of times, and you will understand why police data look as they do. Furthermore, if criminals are disproportionately black and Latino, so will be parolees and probationers. Police can search parolees and probationers after stopping them to make sure that they are complying with the terms of their release and not carrying contraband. Without doubt, a portion of the searches in the LAPD data represents multiple encounters with this particular population, though the data are too crude to identify how large it is.

Where the Crime Is

And where is criminal activity taking place? Nearly half of all homicides in 2001 occurred in South-Central, and slightly more than half of them were gang-related, according to the

Police Department. It stands to reason that homicide investigators will spend a disproportionate amount of time there, where African Americans and Latinos predominate. It is not racism that sends them there; it is the incidence of crime. Would cop bashers prefer that officers investigating a murder on Western Avenue go to Brentwood for the sake of racial balance?

Once in South-Central, the police will probably look for homicide suspects among gang members. If a cop spots a driver flashing gang signs after running a red light, the man will probably be asked to step out of his car when stopped and, if exhibiting suspicious behavior, frisked. Police investigating a murder spree by the Aryan Brotherhood in the Foothill Division would do the same if they spotted a white driver behaving similarly.

Rates of lawbreaking are just the start of what's needed to analyze police activity. Many other details—including patterns of police deployment, relative number of young people in various populations, locations of high-profile crimes and prevalence of illegal immigrants lacking driver's licenses—are also important.

The reemergence of racial-profiling charges following the release of the LAPD data could not have come at a worse moment for the city. The many law-abiding residents in crime-plagued neighborhoods are crying out for protection from the escalating violence. Go to any police-community meeting in a crime-ridden area and the most frequent complaint you will hear is "Why aren't there more cops getting dealers and gang-bangers off the streets?" rather than "Why are you profiling us?"

Sure, some L.A. officers antagonize civilians with their unnecessarily aggressive attitudes, and the department must teach them communications skills and courtesy. But that is a far different problem than endemic officer racism.

Still, if critics keep accusing officers of bigotry for trying in good faith to do their jobs, it will be all the harder for them to fight crime.

> *"Deployment of tasers, rather than minimizing the use of force, may dangerously extend the boundaries of what are considered 'acceptable' levels of force."*

The Use of Tasers Should Be Suspended

Amnesty International

In the following viewpoint Amnesty International argues that electroshock devices, or Tasers, are used abusively by law-enforcement officers. Citing many deaths related to these devices, the organization calls for Taser use to be suspended until an impartial study of their use and effects can be made. Amnesty International is a worldwide organization that promotes human rights and opposes cruel treatment of prisoners.

As you read, consider the following questions:

1. What is one of the built-in product safeguards on Tasers that law-enforcement agencies say minimize the weapon's potential for abuse, according to Amnesty International?

Amnesty International, "Excessive and Lethal Force? Amnesty International's Concerns about Deaths and Ill-Treatment Involving Police Use of Tasers," www.amnestyusa.org, 2004. Reproduced by permission.

2. What are the several types of individuals who have been targeted by police Tasers, according to the authors?

3. What does Amnesty International recommend for U.S. law-enforcement agencies that refuse to stop using Tasers pending an impartial review?

> *"I asked Borden to lift up his foot to remove the shorts, but he was being combative and refused. I dry stunned Borden in the lower abdominal area. . . . We got Borden into the booking area. Borden was still combative and uncooperative. I dried [sic] stunned Borden in the buttocks area. . . ." After the final shock, the officer "noticed that Borden was no longer responsive and his face was discoloured."*
>
> *(extract from officer's statement on James Borden, a mentally disturbed man being booked into an Indiana jail.)*

James Borden was arrested in a disoriented state in November 2003 and died shortly after the administration of the last of six electro-shocks, delivered while his hands were reportedly cuffed behind his back. The medical examiner released a statement listing cause of death as a heart attack, drug intoxication and electrical shock. James Borden is one of thousands of individuals shocked with stun devices by US law enforcement agents each year as a growing number of agencies move to adopt such weapons.

Tasers

More than 5,000 US law enforcement agencies are currently deploying tasers, dart-firing electro-shock weapons designed to cause instant incapacitation by delivering a 50,000 volt shock. Tasers are hand-held electronic stun guns which fire two barbed darts up to a distance of 21 feet, which remain attached to the gun by wires. The fish-hook like darts are designed to penetrate up to two inches of the target's clothing or skin and deliver a high-voltage, low amperage, electro-shock along insulated copper wires. Although they were first introduced in the 1970s, the take-up rate for tasers has increased enormously in recent years, with the marketing of powerful "new generation" models such as the M26 Advanced Taser and the Taser X26. Both fire darts which strike the subject from a distance or, as in James Borden's case, can be applied directly to the skin as a stun gun.

The manufacturers and law enforcement agencies deploying tasers maintain that they are a safer alternative to many conventional weapons in controlling dangerous or combative individuals. Some police departments claim that injuries to officers and suspects, as well as deaths from police firearms, have fallen since their introduction.

Human Rights Concerns

Amnesty International acknowledges the importance of developing non-lethal or "less than lethal" force options to decrease the risk of death or injury inherent in the use of firearms or other impact weapons such as batons. However, the use of stun technology in law enforcement raises a number of concerns for the protection of human rights. Portable and easy to use, with the capacity to inflict severe pain at the push of a button without leaving substantial marks, electro-shock weapons are particularly open to abuse by unscrupulous officials, as the organization has documented in numerous cases around the world.

Although US law enforcement agencies stress that training and in-built product safeguards (such as chips which can record the time and date of each taser firing) minimize the potential for abuse, Amnesty International believes that these safeguards do not go far enough. There have been disturbing reports of inappropriate or abusive use of tasers in various US jurisdictions, sometimes involving repeated cycles of electroshocks.

There is also evidence to suggest that, far from being used to avoid lethal force, many US police agencies are deploying tasers as a routine force option to subdue non-compliant or

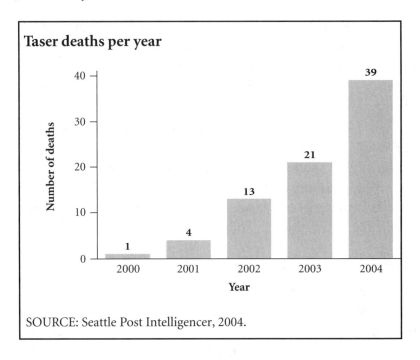

Taser deaths per year

SOURCE: Seattle Post Intelligencer, 2004.

disturbed individuals who do not pose a serious danger to themselves or others. In some departments, tasers have become the most prevalent force tool. They have been used against unruly schoolchildren; unarmed mentally disturbed or intoxicated individuals; suspects fleeing minor crime scenes and people who argue with police or fail to comply immediately with a command. Cases . . . include the stunning of a 15-year-old schoolgirl in Florida, following a dispute on a bus, and a 13-year-old girl in Arizona, who threw a book in a public library.

Deaths Involving Tasers

In many such instances, the use of electro-shock weapons appears to have violated international standards prohibiting torture or other cruel, inhuman or degrading treatment as well as standards set out under the United Nations (UN) Code of Conduct for Law Enforcement Officials and the Basic Principles on the Use of Force and Firearms by Law Enforcement

Officials. These require that force should be used as a last resort and that officers must apply only the minimum amount of force necessary to obtain a lawful objective. They also provide that all use of force must be proportionate to the threat posed as well as designed to avoid unwarranted pain or injury.

International standards encourage the development of non-lethal incapacitating weapons for law enforcement "for use in appropriate situations, with a view to increasingly restraining the application of means capable of causing death or injury to persons" but state that such weapons must be "carefully evaluated" and their use "carefully controlled". Amnesty International believes that this standard has not been met with regard to tasers, despite their increasing use across the country.

Amnesty International is further concerned by the growing number of fatalities involving police tasers. Since 2001, more than 70 people are reported to have died in the USA and Canada after being struck by M26 or X26 tasers, with the numbers rising each year. While coroners have tended to attribute such deaths to other factors (such as drug intoxication), some medical experts question whether the taser shocks may exacerbate a risk of heart failure in cases where persons are agitated, under the influence of drugs, or have underlying health problems such as heart disease. In at least five recent cases, coroners have found the taser directly contributed to the death, along with other factors such as drug abuse and heart disease. . . . [The] death toll heightens Amnesty International's concern about the safety of stun weapons and the lack of rigorous, independent testing as to their medical effects.

[Amnesty International has reviewed] 74 taser-involved deaths, based on a range of sources, including autopsy reports in 21 cases. Most of those who died were unarmed men who, while displaying disturbed or combative behaviour, did not appear to present a serious threat to the lives or safety of others. Yet many were subjected to extreme levels of force, including repeated taser discharges and in some cases dangerous restraint techniques such as "hogtying" (shackling an individual by the wrists and ankles behind their back). The cases raise serious concern about the overall levels of force deployed by some police agencies as well the safety of tasers.

Tasers have been described by many police departments as "filling a niche" on the force scale. However, Amnesty International is concerned that deployment of tasers, rather than minimizing the use of force, may dangerously extend the boundaries of what are considered "acceptable" levels of force. While the organization concedes that there may be limited circumstances under which tasers might be considered an alternative to deadly force, there is evidence to suggest that measures such as stricter controls and training on the use of force and firearms can be more effective in reducing unnecessary deaths or injuries. . . .

Amnesty International is reiterating its call on federal, state and local authorities and law enforcement agencies to suspend all transfers and use of electro-shock weapons, pending an urgent rigorous, independent and impartial inquiry into their use and effects.

Where US law enforcement agencies refuse to suspend tasers, the organization is recommending that their use of tasers is strictly limited to situations where the alternative under international standards would be deadly force, with detailed reporting and monitoring procedures.

> *"Tasers are working. Every day we receive stories of how these devices save lives."*

Tasers Prevent Excessive Force

Rick Smith

Rick Smith asserts in the following viewpoint that electroshock devices, or Tasers, reduce excessive force and prevent deaths because they provide a nonviolent way to subdue suspects. He claims that Tasers have now been modified in response to concerns from critics. One modification is that the devices now record the time and date when fired, increasing police accountability, he asserts. This viewpoint was originally given as a statement in a debate with Bill Schulz, executive director of Amnesty International, a human-rights group that has called for the suspension of use of electroshock weapons such as Tasers until they are thoroughly investigated. Smith is the cofounder and chief executive officer of Taser International, the manufacturer of the Taser device.

As you read, consider the following questions:

1. How do Tasers use electricity to incapacitate someone as harmlessly as possible, according to Smith?

Rick Smith, "Taser International/Amnesty International Debate," held at Claremont McKenna College in Claremont, California, on March 9, 2005. Transcript posted on the Web site of Taser International, http://www.taser.com. Reproduced by permission.

2. What does the author claim Taser technology is designed to uphold?

3. In what two ways does Taser International build accountability into its devices, according to Smith?

I have a tremendous respect for Amnesty International. . . .

As I look at [the debate] tonight I think it's more important that we focus on our common ideals, which far outnumber those that set us apart. In fact I recently learned that (Peter Benenson) formed Amnesty International in 1961 after reading about two students who were arrested in Lisbon for toasting to liberty, while in 1993 I formed Taser International out of a personal experience where two friends of mine were gunned down at a red light [in] Scottsdale, Arizona, where a road-rage incident took their lives and ruined the life of another person who lost his temper and had a gun in the glove box.

Technology Can Do Better

At the time, I started to read about this topic, and I learned that in 1991 over 37,000 Americans died from bullet wounds. Just to put that in perspective, that's more people every two years than we lost in ten years in jungle warfare in Vietnam. It's a big issue.

And looking at it, I said why is it that sitting here today in the early 1990s we're still defending ourselves the way we fought the British in the revolutionary war 200 years ago? Certainly technology can do better.

Now my background was in neurobiology and so the approach that I selected was one called the Taser. It had been around for a while and I picked up the ball from a 73-year-old inventor to take it forward.

Just so you understand what a Taser does: Before the Taser, the way people defend themselves is twofold. One is the brutal process of killing someone by striking them with a bullet. The other non-lethal alternatives all involved pain, whether I hit you with a chemical spray that causes a burning sensation or I hit you with a baton or a club that bruises, causes contusions, breaks bones—it causes pain.

Temporary Impairment

The idea of a Taser is to incapacitate someone as harmlessly as we can. And the method we use is electricity. Now some people think electricity is dangerous but in fact electricity is necessary for the life process. You can't think without it, you can't breathe without it.

Sitting here today, right now there are electric signals running down from my brain, through my spinal cord, and out through nerve trunks into my arm telling my muscles how to move. What we do with a Taser is we plug electrodes into the human body and we flood it with electrical signals that contract those muscles uncontrollably.

It's as if you and I are on a telephone talking and a third party gets on the line and speaks so loud we can't hear each other anymore. But when they get off it didn't damage the phone lines just like the Taser doesn't damage the body. It causes a temporary impairment of communication. So it's really as nonviolent as you can be and yet incapacitate someone and bring a violent situation under control.

Now I mentioned we share a common commitment in the vision of protecting human rights of . . . citizens, law enforcement, and the suspects that they have to deal with. Like many here this evening we also share Amnesty's support for the Universal Declaration of Human Rights and the United Nations Code of Conduct for Law Enforcement, which I think is interesting.

This code states that whenever lawful use of force and firearms is unavoidable, law enforcement shall minimize dam-

Monitoring Taser Use

The [Seattle Police] Department has been carefully monitoring taser use since the first devices were deployed in December 2000.

[The department found that] in only seven cases were injuries to subjects reported and these consisted primarily of superficial marks or welts. Generally, subjects were cleared for booking either at the scene or at the hospital where they had been treated. The only subjects admitted to the hospital were those involuntarily committed for mental health evaluation. Officers were reported injured in two cases.

Seattle Police Department,
Use of Force by Seattle Police Department Officers,
November 2001.

age and injury and respect and preserve human life. That's exactly what our technology is designed to do.

Also we share your concern with preventing death. Any death in police custody is one too many. That's why we're proud to have changed law enforcement for the better and we're saving lives every day.

In fact on our web site at Taser.com you can download 600 documented incidents where a Taser was used to save someone's life. And we know there are thousands more. So Tasers are working. Every day we receive stories of how these devices save lives. I'll give you a couple of examples.

Real-Life Successes

In the past week we received input about a 14-year-old young man in Missouri who had badly beaten his mother. When police showed up at the house he approached them with a Samurai sword. He backed police into a corner, approached them stating, "I'm going to kill you like a ninja."

Two officers—one had a gun, one had a Taser. The officer with the Taser fired, the young man was dropped, his life was surely saved. We received feedback that they certainly would have used lethal force had they not had the Taser, and his mother thanked them for sparing her son's life.

Or another one—(Ed Welch) in California, a knife-wielding subject who approached police urging them to shoot him. He tried to commit suicide by cop. They used a Taser, safely subdued him, and he thanked them afterwards. When he came to his senses he said, "I tried to kill myself, and thank you for not pulling the gun."

Now let's talk about what happens when Tasers are not present. (Theresa Hillman), a police officer in Madison, Wisconsin, doing her duty: She pulls up on a car with an intoxicated driver. A very large, I believe roughly 300-pound male gets out. An altercation ensues.

She tries to subdue him with pepper spray, no effect. She strikes him with a baton, I believe around a dozen times, no effect. He throws her to the ground, jumps on top of her, and pummels her in the face and body with his fist. She sustained injuries so severe it required hospitalization.

When backup arrived he was tugging at her gun trying to get it out of the holster. (Theresa) believes had the backup been seconds later she'd be dead today. She spoke to the Madison City Council and said you cannot take my Taser away. I will not go through that again. Had I had a Taser that night I would not have endured that ordeal.

And in fact each year 58,000 police officers share similar ordeals. And over 80% of them are assaulted by people that are not armed. In fact police can't go through a situation where nobody is armed. They have a gun on them all the time. There's no such thing as a police fight that doesn't involve a weapon.

Built-in Accountability

Now Amnesty has expressed continued concerns about police accountability, and one thing I'd like to say is we've heard you. We listened. When we developed these Tasers we built in tracking systems to increase accountability. We're the only company in the world that makes ammunition that when you fire it, it disperses ID tags back to the registered user.

The other thing that we did was we built into these weapons computer systems that record the time and date every time the trigger is pulled. So the idea is we want to make sure that if officers are misusing the product that they're held accountable, that the agency can download that data. This is a level of accountability presently in no other weapon on earth and we're proud of that record. But I regret to say we haven't received any accolades. So far it's all been criticism.

You know, I met with representatives of Amnesty International in Washington. I've personally flown to [its headquarters in] London. We've extended ourselves and we've made invitations. We want so badly to work with you because we share your goals.

A year ago I invited Amnesty International to send representatives to training because they've expressed concerns about how police are trained with our weapon. A year later, no one has come. Over nine months ago I publicly challenged Amnesty International to co-sponsor a medical study with us. They've certainly been vocal about the shortcomings they see in existing medical science.

So we—I'm sorry, we want to work with you but the silence has been deafening. We have received no protocol that would satisfy your concerns and no offer to cooperate. So tonight I'd like to join—like you to join me in developing better training programs, in developing more effective guidelines, and supporting constructive research that can answer your concerns.

There is no moratorium on crime. Crime won't take a time out. You're talking about a moratorium on Tasers, but we can't stop the world while we work through these issues. We support more research, but every day you take this alternative out of the hands of those who serve, you put lives of officers in jeopardy and you put the lives of suspects in jeopardy.

In fact the Force Research Science Center at the University of Minnesota said that a moratorium, even temporary, with Tasers would be a humanitarian disaster for law enforcement and subjects. It would lead to the death of thousands—I'm sorry, thousands of unnecessary injuries and tens if not hundreds of deaths.

So while cities like Cincinnati and Orange County [California] have cut lethal force, suspect injuries, police injuries by over 50% with the Taser, they have received no positive feedback from Amnesty International nor has any equipment provider like us received any positive feedback for the efforts that we have made to make our weapons responsible. And I can say if all we hear is criticism, people will stop listening.

| "The success of community policing lies in the development of trust-based partnerships between law-enforcement agencies, local government officials, and citizens."

Community Policing Reduces Police Brutality

Edward A. Flynn

Community policing involves a community's residents working with local officials and police to reduce crime and police brutality. Edward A. Flynn asserts in the following viewpoint that community policing helps to foster trusting relationships between law-enforcement officers and community members. Flynn offers a personal history of his working life as a policeman to illustrate the effectiveness of community policing. From being reviled as a young officer by the people he was trying to protect, he eventually came to understand these people better and to earn their respect. Flynn, a former police chief, is the secretary of public safety for the state of Massachusetts.

As you read, consider the following questions:

1. According to James Q. Wilson and George Kelling, as cited by Flynn, what matters most to neighborhood safety?

Edward A. Flynn, "Community Policing: The Past, Present, and Future," police forum.mn-8.net, November 2004. Reproduced by permission.

2. According to the community policing philosophy described by Flynn, how can police deal effectively with crime and disorder?

3. How were approval ratings of the police affected after community policing efforts in Chelsea, Massachusetts, according to the author?

Community policing reduces crime, helps minimize fear of crime, and enhances the quality of life in communities nationwide. The success of community policing lies in the development of trust-based partnerships between law enforcement agencies, local government officials, and citizens. It is a collaborative effort in which law enforcement and community members identify, prioritize, and address crime and disorder problems. The result is strong and confident communities.

Community policing recognizes that the police cannot effectively deal with crime and disorder by only reacting to individual incidents. It broadens the police mandate beyond narrow goals of *law enforcement* as an end in itself. It recognizes the importance of the police in developing and maintaining the idea of "community." To explain why community policing is so important to police leaders of my generation, I begin by telling my story.

A Rookie Cop

In 1971 I began my police career with high ideals. I firmly believed that every U.S. resident was either a part of the problem or a part of the solution. American cities were in a state of crisis, and I wanted to make a difference. My police work provided me with a strong sense of satisfaction, even though I experienced varying degrees of frustration. I quickly understood why police officers become cynical. They deal with human degradation and learn that people are capable of true evil. This experience can erode the idealism of even the most naïve rookie cop.

Despite my best intentions, I was frequently reviled by the same people I was trying to protect. As I worked what was then called a "ghetto" precinct, I was not only exposed to great human need, I also felt for the first time in my life that I was hated for being a police officer. It was unnerving. The community demanded we do something about crime, but when we responded with conventional police tactics, that very same community accused us of harassment. No matter how many arrests we made, crime continued to escalate. No matter how many "sweeps" or "crack downs" we undertook, neighborhoods continued to deteriorate. No matter how fast we got to calls, no matter how many calls we answered, no matter how many fights or disorderly groups we broke up or tickets we wrote, things just seemed to get worse. Meanwhile, my fellow officers and I increasingly felt frustrated, isolated, and more than a little resentful. Our morale was further undermined by our growing awareness of the effect partisan politics could have on the police. As city after city fell into poverty and despair, politicians fought over patronage. As the police department struggled with declining resources and increasing demands for service, politicians expected campaign contributions in return for coveted police assignments.

Yet there was some reason to hope. Federal funds were being allocated to assist law enforcement agencies in educating officials. One example was the Law Enforcement Education Program (LEEP). Federal funds helped to create a generation of leaders in law enforcement who would prove more resistant to political pressure and more committed to progressive policing. As I stated to my friends at the time, "As long as you aren't afraid to wear a uniform and work nights, you can own your soul." Further, it seemed that many cities were gradually escaping their [political-]machine-dominated pasts. Scandals, indictments, and trials were replaced by politicians' "reform" administrations. Although reform administrations were often followed by a return of the old order, the reforms nonetheless seemed to accumulate, impeding a complete return to the past. Mayors and their reforms came and went, but the police made little progress. A political reformer might leave a legacy of newly constructed office buildings and malls, yet some neighborhoods continued their steady decline.

Broken Windows Theory

Back in 1982, while a member of a street-crime unit (a plain-clothes unit specializing in stakeouts and decoy operations), I was greatly influenced by an *Atlantic Monthly* article written by James Q. Wilson and George Kelling (1982). It was entitled "Broken Windows: The Police and Neighborhood Safety." Wilson and Kelling made the argument that what police did to control disorderly behavior in the long term has more to do with neighborhood safety than what the police have tried to do to control crime.

They described citizens who were fearful of using their own streets and contributing to their neighborhood's vitality because of what they witnessed and experienced. Most people never experienced crime, but they saw graffiti and garbage in their neighborhoods. They viewed menacing youths hanging out on the corner; they were accosted by drunken and disturbed panhandlers; and they were propositioned by prostitutes. These behaviors led them to abandon their streets. Next, predators moved into the neighborhoods and, inevitably, serious crime rose as criminals were emboldened by the disorder they saw. Another neighborhood had deteriorated and was gone.

The observations in the article absolutely matched my own experience. We in the police profession were always husbanding our limited resources to deal with serious crimes: robberies, burglaries, rapes, and assaults. We did not have the time for the "minor stuff," even though it was the minor stuff we always heard about from residents. As my precinct captain once said, "When I go to community meetings I never hear any complaints about bank robberies. I do hear complaints about noisy kids, loud music, and disorderly groups."

Was it possible the police could do something to save our neighborhoods? Despite years of efforts to heighten police efficiency to "fight crime," years that had seen the police perfect the tactics of random mobile patrols, rapid response to calls, and follow-up investigations, cities were in continued decline. Furthermore, research was demonstrating that random patrol produced random results; rapid response to crimes did not significantly affect arrest rates; and most criminal investigations were fruitless. Even though the jails were full, it was clear that there was no police solution to the crime problem and no way that the police alone could save the neighborhoods from themselves.

A Quiet Revolution

During the 1980s, what was described as the "Quiet Revolution" in American policing began to emerge. Police agencies soon came to realize that although traditional policing tactics would continue to generate seemingly impressive statistics, they would not, in fact, improve the quality of life in neighborhoods. Strategies designed to resolve this problem were evolving, such as "problem-oriented policing," "neighborhood policing," and "community policing." These terms may be phrased and defined somewhat differently, but they all share common elements that would advance the delivery of police services to all members of our communities.

"Community policing" was not a new idea by any means, but one that had been emerging for years. The community policing philosophy includes two important assumptions. First, the most effective barrier against crime and disorder is a healthy and self-confident neighborhood. Second, police officers are an untapped creative resource in most police departments who are ready and willing to develop practical solutions to neighborhood problems by forming trust-based

The Success of "Hot Spots"

[In 1997] in Maryland, thirty-six neighborhoods formally became "Hot Spots" —one in each county that together accounted for 11 percent of the state's violent crime. In each "Hot Spot" a locally-developed strategy guides both state and local resources. One common feature has been the creation of community-based teams of police and probation officers, jointly supervising high-risk adult and juvenile offenders. . . .

"Hot Spots" seems to be working. . . . Robberies dropped by two-thirds in an Anne Arundel County neighborhood. Overall violent crime dropped by 25 percent in a Wicomico County neighborhood. Among other "Hot Spots," drug market activity dropped in Easton, burglary and theft were cut sharply in Edgewood, and vandalism, robbery, and auto theft went down quickly in Mt. Ranier.

Democratic Leadership Council, "Idea of the Week,"
http://www.dlc.org/ndol_ci.cfm?contentid=1727
&kaid;=119&subid;=213.

partnerships within the community. Community policing recognizes the preeminence of the police role in apprehending criminals and providing emergency services. It also recognizes that the police cannot effectively deal with crime and disorder by only reacting to individual incidents. Along with enlisting community support, the police learn to recognize problems that lead to criminal conditions, and they develop solutions to those particular problems.

I attended my first conference on community policing in Arlington, Virginia, while I was the police chief in Chelsea, Massachusetts. Back then, Chelsea was in state-imposed receivership as the result of a corruption scandal and the city's bankruptcy. This conference interested me because the topic of how community policing could improve the quality of life in distressed cities was being discussed. I was in the process of implementing a community-oriented strategy, and I was emphasizing to my officers its potential to "bring down the crime, the disorder, and the 'for sale' signs." In a city where politics had been a problem, I was giving them this message: "Before, the politicians inserted themselves between the police and the community. Now the community will be between the police and the politicians." . . .

Community Policing After September 11

Community policing is more important now than ever. After [the September 11, 2001, terrorist attacks] homeland security issues (preventing and responding to terrorist acts as well as community stabilization) became law enforcement's primary focus. These issues are issues of local and national importance. Although terrorists may "think globally," they "act locally." I was the chief in Arlington County, Virginia, and was among the first responders to the Pentagon, which is located in that county, after it was hit by a hijacked plane. I have been immersed in homeland security issues for some time. Through the many briefings on resource allocations, new technologies, interoperability, and other plans to counter the new terrorist threats, I remain convinced that one of the greatest weapons against terrorists is community policing. A vital component of community policing requires law enforcement and communities to work together, to connect with one another, and establish trust. Across the country there are many *communities of interest* with respect to the fight against terrorism. While some are clearly defined geographically as districts or neighborhoods, others are defined by race or ethnicity. For example, Arlington County has the most diverse zip code in the D.C.-metropolitan area. After Spanish, the second most frequently spoken foreign language is Amharic (spoken by Ethiopians). I know that Arlington County is not alone in its struggle to overcome the challenges that will result in better services to diverse communities.

Law enforcement officials appreciate that residents provide information only when they trust the police. There have been instances when members of the community who have provided law enforcement with information about crime have put themselves at great personal risk, particularly in regard to drug dealing cases and homicides. It is not difficult to imagine that some communities are privy to information they could share regarding terrorist activities or cells. If they trusted law enforcement, they would be more inclined to cooperate with officials and provide them with critical information regarding terrorists and other threats. If community members believe that the police are *their* police and not just *the* police, they will become partners in the war on terrorism as well as the war on crime. . . .

Communities First

It was about 1992, as the police chief of Chelsea, Massachusetts, that I saw the promise of community policing. It was there in Chelsea, with the assistance of [social programs] Weed and Seed and COPS grants, that I first implemented a strategy based on partnerships with the community as well as problem solving, crime prevention, geographic accountability, and officer empowerment. As a result of community policing efforts, the crime rate in Chelsea decreased, officers' job satisfaction increased, citizens' approval ratings of the police improved, and the city evolved from state-imposed receivership to designation as an All-American City by the National Civic League.

In 1997 I was appointed the police chief in Arlington County. In many ways Arlington was the antithesis of the Chelsea I knew. Arlington County's political environment was stable, its local government practice was very professional, and its police force was the longest and continually CALEA [Commission on Accreditation for Law-Enforcement Agencies]-accredited agency in the country. The community policing strategy had great power and promise in Arlington—a community experiencing rapid demographical diversification. Four years after community policing became the dominant strategy there, a decentralized, community policing model was in place that emphasized partnerships, problem solving, crime prevention, officer empowerment, and geographical accountability. As a result of employing the community policing model, the Arlington County Police Department had a very high approval rating, and twenty-year lows in crime when I left in January 2003.

As a police chief making my first attempt to implement community policing, I can recall the rolling of the eyes and the crossed arms over chests of doubting and unconvinced officers. I attended many conferences on the subject of what the true definition of community policing was, and whether or not it qualified as something new and innovative. A decade later, the bulk of my patrol force in Arlington County had known no other strategy than community policing. Yes, they still like to respond rapidly to emergency calls. Yes, they still enjoy the thrill of a good "pinch." But police officers, managers, and chief executives all understand their responsibilities.

The development of trust-based partnerships in neighborhoods, the critical importance of problem solving, and collaborative problem identification remain central components of crime control efforts. Ten years from now, when data from 1994 to 2014 are assessed, what will be measured will not be "community" policing but rather "good" policing because it will finally be evident that policing *is* about communities.

> *"Unofficial videos are increasingly orga-*
> *nized by the public itself and have be-*
> *come a tool of civil society for watching*
> *the state."*

Video Monitoring Reduces Police Brutality

Dominique Wisler

In the following viewpoint Dominique Wisler asserts that home videos can be powerful tools for curtailing police brutality. Citizens have captured brutal police actions at crime scenes and protests. Wisler contends that these tapes prompt police departments to significantly increase their accountability to the public. Wisler is a police consultant in Geneva, Switzerland.

As you read, consider the following questions:

1. How does the author assess the "rough" quality of amateur videos?

2. What message does the Belgian political group mentioned by Wisler distribute on tracts during their twenty-four-hour surveillance of the police?

3. How do courts of law regard videos submitted as evidence, according to Wisler?

Dominique Wisler, *Media in Security and Governance: The Role of the News Media in Security Oversight and Accountability.* Baden-Baden, Germany: 2004. Reproduced by permission.

A new development [in public scrutiny of law enforcement] is the increased visibility of police through what I would call unofficial media or videos. The most famous illustration is certainly the Rodney King beating videotape. The videotape shows [according to researchers Skolnick and Fify]: "a large black man down on hands and knees, struggling on the ground, twice impaled with wires from an electronic TASER gun, rising and falling while being repeatedly beaten, blow after blow—dozens of blows, fifty-six in all, about the head, neck, back, kidneys, ankles, legs, feet—by two police officers wielding their 2-foot black metal truncheons like baseball bats. Also visible was a third officer, who was stomping King, and about ten police officers watching the beating along with a number of . . . neighbors." The 90-second videotape was seen repeatedly on CNN giving it national and international exposure.

Unofficial Video

The unofficial video is different from the "official" camera of the journalist profession in several respects that create, in my opinion, a new dynamic in policing. What are these differences?

- First of all, while official media images are produced by a class of intermediaries (the profession of journalists), videotapes are produced directly by the public. Official media pages are the *public eye* while anonymous video the *public's eyes*. They are pictures taken by anonymous individuals from the public directly and not from the professional class of the journalists. They have this directness of character that seemingly represents the point of view of the public, a factor that increases dramatically their credibility.

- Second, the video, contrary to what is often the case with the official camera, does not capture a staged event (constructed for the official camera by professionals of public relations in the police), but they capture uncontrolled *low-visibility activities where, arguably, rank-and-file* subculture play an important role. This uncontrollable character shows the limits of public relations in their case.

- Thirdly the amateur video produces a different kind of material, often a relatively bad quality of light, angle, speed, etc., which resembles the material obtained from a hidden camera or, at best, a TV reality show. These images symbolize the roughness, bumpiness and the crudeness of reality itself. These images stimulate a sense of veracity, a sense of a reality that is kept hidden from the public, that is private. The medium here is the message.

Video Activists

An important development is that the unofficial videos are increasingly organized by the public itself and have become a tool of civil society for watching the state. Indeed, recently, social movements have organized themselves to monitor (with videos) police action with the so-called video activists. The antiglobalization movement of the late nineties has been instrumental in diffusing the concept and the practice of "video activism" or vigilantism. Video activists follow public protests and film the action from every angle, focusing particularly on police (mis)behaviour. Video activists today are organized in collectives in many cities in the Western world. The world wide web and alternative media centres are used as a tool for diffusion of the videotapes and as a resource for advice on the use of videotapes. . . .

With the popularisation of cheap video gear—a Hi-8 analogue camera costs $300 while a digital one (whose pictures can be edited easily on a PC) starts at about $600—and PC editing software and their increased use by organized social groups, the vulnerability of police to public opinion has reached a paroxysm.

On the web site of the video activist network, several reasons are underlined for protest organizers to videotape the action during the event:

- Video Activism deters police violence.

- Video Activism helps to document what occurs at actions, for legal follow-up purposes.

- Video Activism doesn't water-down, or alter the message of the people.

- Video Activism allows the people themselves to shape public debate about our world of multiple crises, articulating what is truly relevant news about the world we share. The huge number of people who have their own video cameras at demonstrations today is testament to the democratization of electronic communications.

- Video Activism is a big feature of the growing world of independent media. More and more concerned people, all over the world, are actually making their own media and by-passing the established, corporate-owned press with their own stories and their unique visions of a better world.

Cameras Are Watching

A recent example [of video activism] is a radical Islamic group, the Arab European League (AEL), in Anvers, Belgium. The group organized 24-hour surveillance beat teams equipped with videos and digital cameras watching the police. They distribute tracts which claim *"Bad cops, AEL is watching you."*

Apart from the Rodney King videotape, there are many examples of unofficial cameras capturing rank-and-file misbehaviour. Let me mention a few cases, some of them involv-[ing] video surveillance tapes of the police themselves:

- McDonald and Paromchik mention the case of a high-way patrolman driving in an unmarked car that was equipped with a video camera whose intended use was to document how the suspect behaved during the arrest, particularly useful in drunk driving arrests and resisting arrests. However, it caught a police officer who dragged a woman out of her car and roughed her up after a long chase during which she refused to pull over.

- Another example involves a prison in Japan. Five prison guards have been charged on account of brutal behaviour with a detainee. They had placed a detainee in a isolation cell and compressed his stomach with a leather belt so tightly that the man needed a surgical intervention. The director of the prison first denied any wrongdoing, but the event had been taped by the video-surveillance system installed in the prison to prevent [suicides] (see The *Courier International*, no 630, p. 36, November 28 to December 4th 2002).

- Other well publicised cases involve attacking dogs of border guards in South Africa and a Moroccan woman severely beaten by French policemen filmed by an amateur camera.

- Another case involves video footage by video activists in the G8[1] Genoa policing of the antiglobalization rally. *The Wall Street Journal*, September 11, 2001, wrote:

". . . at the recent Group of Eight summit meeting (. . .) Video activists caught on tape several scenes of gratuitous police violence against protesters. The footage of officers us-

1. The Group of Eight consists of eight economic leaders in the world, including the United States.

Video Activists

[In Spring 2001], tens of thousands of anti-capitalist activists descended on the Summit of the Americas in Quebec City. They came from all across North and South America to protest the intended formation of the Free Trade Area of the Americas (FTAA), a multilateral agreement critics argued would bolster trade at the expense of democracy. They wore the usual gas masks and goggles and brandished banners. But amid the chants of protesters in the city's narrow streets, other sounds could be heard: the beeps of hundreds of hand-held video cameras. . . .

Protests have erupted everywhere global trade zealots have tried to assemble, be it the World Trade Organization (WTO) in Prague or the World Economic Forum in Melbourne. These events also mark a resurgence of video activism, and they may well have been the most widely disseminated protests ever. . . .

The IMCs [independent media centres] are part of a loose but rapidly growing network of video activists, or, more broadly, media activists. These high tech activists use video to challenge the mainstream media, to disseminate, information and news about events that are otherwise marginalized or not covered, to propagandize, and to document police abuse.

Rachel Rinaldo, LiPmagazine.org, 2002.
www.lipmagazine.org.

ing truncheons and tear gas on peaceful demonstrators—including elderly women with their hands raised in gestures of submission—quickly whirred around the globe on the Internet. Soon, the tapes were picked up by Italy's main TV networks, prompting a public outcry and a criminal investigation of police behavior."

What Consequences?

The unofficial video has brought the intensity of the spotlight of the media and the public to a new height. Traditional low visibility activities cannot [be hidden] anymore from the camera, pictures are less negotiable, the vulnerability to the public has increased dramatically. Moreover, the quality of the video pictures is sufficient to be broadcast by television networks and be accessible by the mass public. These pictures are also admissible in courts as evidence.

All these features intensify the pressure on the police and encourage them to reform in two directions: first, to increase mechanisms of internal control in order to increase [restraint] and second, to play the card of transparency.

The fear of the camera has been traditionally a tool for the management to increase their control over the behaviour of rank-and-file. Training is another tool in this regard. As far as I can see, police training has experienced lately a change of focus, from teaching to learning and from teaching "theory" to learning "skills". The emphasis is less on legal and theoretical knowledge than on practical skills and on mastering the correct behaviour in a given situation. Police students learn these skills in simulations of the situation, teachers become coaches of students and skills are learnt in interdisciplinary modules (team teaching) around a situation (arrest, control, etc.).

The tendency seems also to be on bringing deontology [the belief that the correctness of an action lies within itself, not in the consequences of the action] into training. Within the new pedagogy described above, deontology becomes an essential skill to be acquired. The advantage of this type of training is to move from learning theoretical "conventions" and codes to acquiring practical deontological skills and, therefore, reducing the vulnerability of police to the media. . . .

Police Transparency

Better external accountability and more transparency is another answer to the intensified public scrutiny. I expect police to open up voluntarily even more to public scrutiny. At an antiglobalization rally in 1999, the Geneva police decided to authorize the public television network to film the preparation of the police for the event and even to put a microphone on the collar of the commanding officer in a protest policing operation. (The event turned violent and the officer gave his instructions live!) The officer explained to me his philosophy in an interview:

> "I want to come back on the fact that . . . we have nothing to hide. [This] presents a problem for those who prefer to believe that the police [force] is silly, stupid, violent, etc., and more and more one has to observe that it is not the case. We have been quite transparent at both levels, the personnel and the mass media. We have nothing to hide."

In a similar vein, a Turkish gendarme explained to me that when they intervene in a Kurdish village they always bring along a video crew who film the action as a means to prevent claims of mishandling. Transparency is the best weapon of the police today in the media game. Still in the same vein, a Swiss officer explained to me that he advocated the use of internal surveillance camera within prisons cells in order to prevent prisoners from making false allegations of abuses.

Periodical Bibliography

The following articles have been selected to supplement the diverse views presented in this chapter.

| Ruben Castenada and Jamie Stockwell | "County Signs On to Curb Alleged Police Abuses," *Washington Post*, January 29, 2004. |

| *Detroit Free Press* | "Ex-Detroit Officer Seeks Conviction Reversal in Fatal Beating," April 9, 2005. |

| James Forman Jr. | "Community Policing and Youth as Assets," *Journal of Criminal Law and Criminology*, Fall 2004. |

| Harvey Gee | "The First Amendment and Police Misconduct: Criminal Penalty for Filing Complaints Against Police Officers," *Hamline Law Review*, Spring 2004. |

| *Jet* | "Videotaped Beating of Teen in Inglewood, CA, Sparks Lawsuit, Federal Probe, and Nationwide Outrage," July 29, 2002. |

| Asit S. Panwala | "The Failure of Local and Federal Prosecutors to Curb Police Brutality," *Fordham Urban Law Journal*, January 2, 2003. |

| Jeremy W. Peters | "Wrongful Conviction Prompts Detroit Police to Videotape Certain Interrogations," *New York Times*, April 11, 2006. |

| Jessica Snyder Sachs | "DNA and a New Kind of Racial Profiling: Police Sketches from Eyewitness Accounts Are Notoriously Unreliable. The Question Is, Will 'DNA Sketches' Be Any Better?" *Popular Science*, December 2003. |

| Brad W. Smith | "The Impact of Police Officer Diversity on Police-Caused Homicides," *Policy Studies Journal*, May 2003. |

| Susan Sward | "San Francisco Police Monitoring Criticized," *San Francisco Chronicle*, April 21, 2006. |

For Further Discussion

Chapter 1

1. The U.S. Commission on Civil Rights highlights racial profiling of suspects by police and racism by police as the primary reasons for what they see as widespread law-enforcement abuse. In his dissenting opinion, Russell G. Redenbaugh maintains that the commission oversimplifies the issue of police brutality by emphasizing the race issue. He asserts that racism is not the root cause of police brutality. What facts does each viewpoint present to support its argument? Which data are more convincing, and why?

2. Heidi Boghosian asserts that since September 11, 2001, terrorist attacks on the United States, the government's antiterrorist policies have led federal and local police to limit the rights of citizens' free speech and free assembly through means as drastic as "spying" on their activities and using excessive force. Why would a government be compelled to limit public protests during a time when it was battling terrorism? What would be the pros and cons of a government limiting free speech and assembly at such a time?

3. Llewellyn H. Rockwell Jr. claims that police are permitted to break the laws they allegedly enforce. "They are permitted to speed, trespass, and rob in the name of cracking down on speeding, trespassing, and robbing," he writes. Are police justified in breaking the same laws they are trying to enforce? Under what circumstances should it be permissible for the police to be unlawful in upholding laws?

Chapter 2

1. Sundiata Keita Cha-Jua outlines the historical foundation of racism in U.S. law enforcement and cites modern examples of racially motivated police violence. Heather Mac Donald supports her argument that police are not racist by interviewing "several dozen" African American police officers who deny racism among law enforcers. Which argument do you find more convincing: the historical data as interpreted by Cha-Jua or the first-person opinions that Mac Donald cites? Which argument is more objective? Explain your answer.

2. Donald E. Wilkes Jr. discusses what he sees as the inappropriate militarization of U.S. police forces, including the use of stun grenades. These devices emit "a temporarily blinding light and temporarily deafening concussion," but do not propel shrapnel, like a traditional grenade. Though the police classify the devices as "nonlethal," Wilkes maintains that they have been involved in the deaths of at least four suspects after police used them to execute search warrants. Under what circumstances do you believe the police are justified in using such devices? Does the use of such devices constitute "excessive force" against citizens? Explain your answer.

Chapter 3

1. Tim Hames and Emanuele Ottolenghi discuss a July 2005 incident in London in which police shot and killed an innocent man suspected of being a suicide bomber. In an age when one bomb-carrying individual may be capable of killing dozens or more people, are police justified in "shooting to kill" a suspect they believe is a suicide bomber? What kind of factors would have to be present for police to have just cause to kill such a suspect? How many of those factors were present in the London incident?

Chapter 4

1. Heather Mac Donald asserts that racial profiling is effective because it enables police to target the people most likely to commit crimes. If it is true that, for example, more African Americans than white people commit robberies in Los Angeles, are the Los Angeles police justified in using race as a basis for targeting suspects? Explain your answer using data from the viewpoints. Are your conclusions the same when you consider other examples, such as ethnic profiling of travelers at an airport?

2. Rick Smith asserts that electroshock devices, or Tasers, "are saving lives every day," because they allow police to subdue suspects without hurting them. Amnesty International cites more than seventy people who have died since 2001 in North America after being hit with electroshock devices—although coroners tend not to attribute the deaths directly to the devices. Is this proof enough that Tasers and similar devices should be banned until they can be further studied? Which viewpoint presents a better argument, and why? Which author do you perceive as more objective, and why?

3. Dominique Wisler believes that amateur videos of police misconduct, such as the infamous tape of Rodney King being beaten by Los Angeles police officers, have high credibility among the public because of the lack of polish in their presentation. "These images symbolize the roughness, bumpiness and crudeness of reality itself. These images stimulate a sense of veracity, a sense of a reality that is kept hidden from the public." Discuss Wisler's contention: How can such videos affect public opinion of police conduct? Are they a positive or negative force in helping to curb police misconduct?

Organizations to Contact

American Civil Liberties Union (ACLU)
125 Broad St., 18th Foorl., New York, NY   10004-2400
Web site: www.aclu.org

The ACLU is a national organization that works to defend Americans' civil rights guaranteed in the U.S. Constitution. Among other services, the ACLU provides legal assistance to victims of police abuse. The ACLU published *Fighting Police Abuse: A Community Action Manual* in 1997. The 2003 New York Civil Liberties Union report "Arresting Protest" is available at the ACLU Web site.

Amnesty International USA
5 Penn Plaza, 14th Floor., New York, NY   10001
(212) 807-8400 • fax: (212) 627-1451
e-mail: admin-us@aiusa.org
Web site: www.amnestyusa.org

Amnesty International is a worldwide campaigning movement that works to promote human rights and opposes cruel treatment of prisoners. Its reports "Police Brutality and Excessive Force in the New York City Police Department," "Race, Rights, and Police Brutality," and "Cruelty in Control? The Stun Belt and Other Electro-Shock Equipment in Law Enforcement" are available on its Web site.

The Heritage Foundation
214 Massachusetts Ave. NE, Washington, DC   20002-4999
(202) 546-4400 • fax: (202) 546-8328
e-mail: info@heritage.org
Web site: www.heritage.org

The Heritage Foundation is a conservative public policy research institute that advocates strengthening law enforcement to stop crime. It publishes position papers on a broad range of topics, including police issues. Its regular publications include the Backgrounder series of occasional papers and the Heritage Lecture series.

Human Rights Watch

350 Fifth Ave. 34th Floor., New York, NY   10118-3299
(212) 290-4700 • fax: (212) 736-1300
e-mail: hrwnyc@hrw.org
Web site: www.hrw.org

Human Rights Watch monitors and reports human rights abuses in the United States and internationally. It sponsors fact-finding missions, disseminates results, and provides weekly and monthly e-mail newsletters and updates. The report "Shielded from Justice: Police Brutality and Accountability in the United States" is available on its Web site.

International Association of Chiefs of Police (IACP)

515 N. Washington St., Alexandria, VA   22314
(703) 836-6767 • fax: (703) 836-4543
Web site: www.theiacp.org

The IACP consists of police executives who provide consultation, research services, and educational programs for police departments nationwide. The association publishes the monthly *Police Chief* magazine, which covers all aspects of law enforcement. Selected articles and reports are available on its Web site, including "Policies Help Gain Public Trust: Racial Profiling" and "Police Use of Force in America 2001."

Law Enforcement Alliance of America (LEAA)

5538 Port Royal Rd., Springfield, VA   22151
(703) 847-2677
Web site: www.leaa.org

The LEAA is a coalition of law enforcement professionals, crime victims, and concerned citizens united to fight for legislation that reduces violent crime while preserving the rights of all citizens, particularly the right of self-defense. The LEAA publishes the magazine *Shield* and the newsletter *LEAA Advisor*, recent issues of which are available on the LEAA Web site.

National Association for the Advancement of Colored People (NAACP)
4805 Mt. Hope Dr., Baltimore, MD   21215
toll free: (877) NAACP-98
Web site: www.naacp.org

The NAACP is a civil rights organization that works to end racial discrimination in the United States. It researches and documents police brutality and provides legal services for victims of brutality. The NAACP publishes the book *Beyond the Rodney King Story: An Investigation of Police Misconduct in Minority Communities* as well as the magazine *Crisis* ten times per year.

National Black Police Association (NBPA)
3251 Mt. Pleasant St. NW, 2nd Floor.
Washington, DC   20010-2103
(202) 986-2070 • fax: (202) 986-0410
e-mail: nbpanatofc@worldnet.att.net
Web site: www.blackpolice.org

The NBPA is a nationwide organization of African American police associations dedicated to the promotion of justice, fairness, and effectiveness in law enforcement. The organization also serves as an advocate for minority police officers. It publishes "Police Brutality: A Strategy to Stop the Violence."

National Center for Women and Policing (NCWP)
433 S. Beverly Dr., Beverly Hills, CA   90212
(310) 556-2526 • fax: (310) 556-2509
e-mail: womencops@feminist.org
Web site: www.womenandpolicing.org

A division of the Feminist Majority Foundation, the NCWP promotes the increase of numbers of women at all ranks of law enforcement as a strategy to improve police response to violence against women, reduce police brutality and excessive force, and strengthen community policing reforms. The report "Men, Women, and Police Excessive Force: A Tale of Two Genders" is available on the NCWP Web site.

National Coalition on Police Accountability (N-COPA)
407 S. Dearborn St., Suite 1490, Chicago, IL   60605
(312) 663-5392 • fax: (312) 663-5396
e-mail: info@nationalcoalitiononpoliceaccountability.org
Web site: http://nationalcoalitiononpoliceaccountability.org

N-COPA is an organization of religious, community, and legal groups and of progressive law enforcement representatives working to hold police accountable to their communities through public education, community organization, legislation, litigation, and the promotion of empowered independent oversight.

National Institute of Justice (NIJ)
810 Seventh St. NW, Washington, DC   20531
(301) 519-5500
Web site: www.ojp.usdoj.gov/nij

A component of the Office of Justice Programs of the U.S. Department of Justice, the NIJ supports and conducts research on crime, criminal behavior, and crime prevention. The NIJ acts as a clearinghouse for criminal justice information for researchers and other interested individuals. It publishes and distributes the following reports from the Bureau of Justice Statistics: "National Data Collection on Police Use of Force," "The Role of Psychology in Controlling Excessive Force," and "Understanding the Use of Force by and Against the Police."

**National Organization of Black Law
Enforcement Executives (NOBLE)**
Hubert T. Bell Jr. Office Complex
Alexandria, VA   22312-1442
(703) 658-1529 • fax: (703) 658-9479

e-mail: noble@noblenatl.org
Web site: www.noblenatl.org

NOBLE serves the interests of black law enforcement officials. It works to eliminate racism, increase minority participation at all levels of law enforcement, and foster community involvement in working to reduce urban crime and violence. NOBLE condemns the use of excessive force by police. Its publications include the quarterly magazine *NOBLE National* and the newsletter *NOBLE Actions.*

October 22nd Coalition
PO Box 2627, New York, NY   10009
Toll free: 1-888-NO-BRUTALITY
e-mail: office@october22-ny.org
Web site: http://october22-ny.org/national/

The coalition is a diverse group of activist organizations and individuals concerned about police brutality. October 22nd is the date of the coalition's annual National Day of Protest against Police Brutality, Repression, and the Criminalization of a Generation, which is intended to raise awareness about police misconduct. The coalition publishes a newsletter, available online, as part of its efforts to organize protest activities. It also coordinates the Stolen Lives Project, which documents the names of those who have been brutalized and killed by the police since 1990. The coalition also publishes the newsletter *Wear Black!*

Police Executive Research Forum (PERF)
1120 Connecticut Ave. NW, Suite 930
Washington, DC   20036
(202) 466-7820 • fax: (202) 466-7826
e-mail: perf@policeforum.org
Web site: www.policeforum.org

PERF is a national professional association of police executives that seeks to increase public understanding of and stimulate debate on important criminal justice issues. PERF's numerous publications include the book *And Justice for All: Understanding and Controlling Police Abuse of Force* and the papers "The Force Factor: Measuring Police Use of Force Relative to Suspect Resistance" and "Police Use of Force: A Statistical Analysis of the Metro-Dade Police Department."

Police Foundation

2101 Connecticut Ave. NW, Washington, DC   20036-2636
(202) 833-1460 • fax: (202) 659-9149
e-mail: pfinfo@policefoundation.org
Web site: www.policefoundation.org

The foundation conducts research projects on police activities and aims to improve the quality of police personnel. It publishes the report "Officer Behavior in Police-Citizen Encounters: A Descriptive Model and Implications for Less-than-Lethal Alternatives" and the books *Police Use of Force: Official Reports, Citizen Complaints, and Legal Consequences* and *The Abuse of Police Authority: A National Study of Police Officers' Attitudes.*

Bibliography of Books

Bruce Ackerman   *Before the Next Attack: Preserving Civil Liberties in an Age of Terrorism.* New Haven, CT: Yale University Press, 2006.

Geoffrey P. Alpert and Roger G. Dunham   *Understanding Police Use of Force: Officers, Suspects and Reciprocity.* Cambridge, UK: Cambridge University Press, 2004.

Nancy V. Baker   *General Ashcroft: Attorney at War.* Lawrence: University Press of Kansas, 2006.

Kenneth Bolton Jr. and Joe R. Feagin   *Black in Blue: African-American Police Officers and Racism.* New York: Routledge, 2004.

Dean J. Champion   *Police Misconduct in America: A Reference Handbook.* Santa Barbara, CA: ABC-CLIO, 2001.

Christopher Dunn et al.   *Arresting Protest: Special Report of the New York Civil Liberties Union.* New York: American Civil Liberties Union, 2003.

Byrna J. Fireside   *The Trial of the Police Officers in the Shooting Death of Amadou Diallo: A Headline Court Case.* Berkeley Heights, NJ: Enslow, 2004.

William A. Geller and Hans Toch, eds.   *Police Violence: Understanding and Controlling Police Abuse of Force.* New Haven, CT: Yale University Press, 1996.

Edward Humes

Mean Justice: A Town's Terror, a Prosecutor's Power, a Betrayal of Innocence. New York: Simon & Schuster, 2003.

Marilynn S. Johnson

Street Justice: A History of Police Violence in New York City. Boston: Beacon, 2003.

Juan Antonio Juarez

Brotherhood of Corruption: A Cop Breaks the Silence on Police Abuse, Brutality, and Racial Profiling. Chicago: Chicago Review, 2004.

Regina G. Lawrence

The Politics of Force: Media and the Construction of Police Brutality. Berkeley and Los Angeles: University of California Press, 2000.

Kim Michelle Lersch, ed.

Policing and Misconduct. Upper Saddle River, NJ: Prentice-Hall, 2002.

Andrea McArdle and Tanya Erzen, eds.

Zero Tolerance: Quality of Life and the New Police Brutality in New York City. New York: New York University Press, 2001.

William P. McCarney, Gene L. Scaramella, and Steven M. Cox

Contemporary Municipal Policing. Boston: Allyn & Bacon, 2003.

Edwin Meese III and P.J. Ortmeier

Leadership, Ethics, and Policing: Challenges for the 21st Century. Upper Saddle River, NJ: Prentice-Hall, 2004.

Jill Nelson, ed.

Police Brutality: An Anthology. New York: Norton, 2000.

Michael J. Palmiotto, ed. — *Police Misconduct: A Reader for the 21st Century.* Upper Saddle River, NJ: Prentice-Hall, 2001.

Christian Parenti — *The Soft Cage: Surveillance in America from Slavery to the War on Terror.* New York: Basic Books, 2003.

Kenneth J. Peak and Ronald W. Glensor — *Community Policing and Problem Solving: Strategies and Practices.* 4th ed. Upper Saddle River, NJ: Prentice-Hall, 2004.

Joycelyn M. Pollock — *Ethics in Crime and Justice: Dilemmas and Decisions.* Belmont, CA: Wadsworth, 2004.

Michael W. Quinn — *Walking with the Devil: The Police Code of Silence.* Minneapolis: Quinn and Associates, 2004.

Norm Stamper — *Breaking Rank: A Top Cop's Exposé of the Dark Side of American Policing.* New York: Nation Books, 2005.

William Terrill — *Police Coercion: Application of the Force Continuum.* New York: LFB Scholarly, 2001.

Quint C. Thurman and Jihong Zhao — *Contemporary Policing: Controversies, Challenges, and Solutions: An Anthology.* Los Angeles: Roxbury, 2004.

Samuel Walker — *The New World of Police Accountability.* Thousand Oaks, CA: Sage, 2005.

Samuel Walker — *Police Accountability: The Role of Citizen Oversight.* Belmont, CA: Wadsworth, 2005.

| Ronald Weitzer and Steven A. Tuch | *Race and Policing in America: Conflict and Reform*. New York: Cambridge University Press, 2006. |
| Kristian Williams | *Our Enemies in Blue: Police and Power in America*. Brooklyn, NY: Soft Skull Press, 2004. |

Index

Abu Ghraib prison, 89, 90

accountability. *See* discipline

Adams, Eric, 67

African Americans
police officers, 64–69
see also racial profiling; racism

Alito, Samuel A., 119

Alliance for Justice, 119

Amin, Janiil Al-, 56

Amnesty International, 53, 133, 140

Anderson, Bruce, 114

Anderson, William, 124

anti-gay policing, 53–54

Arab European League (AEL), 158

Arlington County, Virginia, 154

Ashcroft, John, 35–36, 40, 43–45

Asian Americans, 23, 57, 124
see also racial profiling

Atlantic Monthly (magazine), 149

Basic Principles on the Use of
Force and Firearms by Law Enforcement Officials (UN), 136–37

Birmingham, Alabama, 19

bisexual Americans, 53–54

Black Panther Party, 60, 61

Boghosian, Heidi, 34

Borden, James, 134, 137–38

Bork, Robert, 121

Borum, Randy, 83

"Broken Windows: The Police and
Neighborhood Safety" (Wilson
and Kelling), 149

Brown, David, 66

Bunch, Kathy, 83

Callahan, Gene, 124

capital punishment, 59–60

Cerbelli, Kevin, 82

Cerbelli, Loretta, 82, 85

Cha-Jua, Sundiata Keita, 55

Chakrabarti, Shami, 107

Chapman, Wilbur, 67–68

Chelsea, Massachusetts, 151–52, 153

Chicago Police Department, 53

Churchill, Winston, 80

Cincinnati Police Department, 47, 145

civilian review panels
are effective in decreasing use
of excessive force, 29
con, 32, 62

civil rights movement, 19

Code of Conduct for Law Enforcement Officials (UN), 136–
37, 141–42

Collins v. Jordan, 39

Commission on Civil Rights, 21, 29

communication skills, importance
of, 32

community policing programs, 29, 147, 149–54

Congressional Black Caucus
(CBC), 61

Congress of Afrikan Peoples, 61

Connor, Eugene "Bull," 19

Constitution
First Amendment
barriers to exercise rights
in, 39–40
Department of Justice does
not protect rights in, 35–
39, 40–45
Fourth Amendment
dynamic entries violate, 79
militarization of police endangers, 74–75
racial profiling and, 124
Section 213 and, 97

Supreme Court decisions about, 97, 101, 118
violations, 37
Fifth Amendment, 37
Fourteenth Amendment, 36
covert entry searches. *See* sneak and peek searches
crime rates, 129
criminal profiles, 126
cultural competence, 31–32

Dalia v. United States, 101
Davis, Robert, 14
Dean, John, 92
death penalty, 59–60
declaratory relief, 43
delayed notice searches. *See* sneak and peek searches
democracies and states of emergency, 113
deontology, 161
Department of Justice
abets police use of excessive force, 62
does not protect free speech, 35–39, 40–45
racial profiling guidelines, 121–23, 125–26
sneak and peek searches are vital to strategy, 100
wartime detention and interrogation tactics and, 89
Diallo, Amadou, 23
discipline
can stop misconduct, 25–26, 32–33
is rare, 61–62
videotapes can provide evidence for, 158, 159
diversity training, 31–32
domestic spying, 38, 40–42
Dorismond, Patrick, 23
Drug Enforcement Agency (DEA), 94, 105, 125

Dunn, Timothy J., 72
Dunne, John, 45
Dutta, Sunil, 31
dynamic entries, 76–80

electro-shock weapons, 134–38, 140–45, 156
equitable relief, 43
evidence
planting, 23
videotapes as, 19–20, 158, 159
executions, 59–60
external controls vs. internal, 32–33

FBI (Federal Bureau of Investigation)
excessive force used, 23
sneak and peek searches, 94
surveillance, 38, 40–42
federalized police. *See* militarization
federal monitors, 32
Fifth Amendment, 37
First Amendment
barriers to exercise rights in, 39–40
Department of Justice does not protect rights in, 35–39, 40–45
Flynn, Edward A., 146
force
discipline and use of, 25–26, 32–33
excessive, 22–23
civil rights protesters and, 19
punishment for, is rare, 62
rules of proportionality, 49–50
shoot-to-kill policies and, 107–10, 112–15

Supreme Court decisions about, 118–19

training and, 14–15, 25–26, 31–32

types of, 56

used against LGBT Americans, 53

used against mentally ill, 82, 85

used against people of color, 60

used against protesters, 39

use of, is decreasing, 25, 29

use of, is increasing, 37, 41, 50, 71–72

videotaping of, 19–20

factors determining use, 29–30

international standards for use, 136–37

intraracial use of, 31

slave codes legalized use of, 58

tasers usage, 134–38, 140–45

transparency of police actions and use of, 162

Force Research Center (University of Minnesota), 145

Forces of Deviance: Understanding the Dark Side of Police (1998 treatise), 74

Forest Service, 124

Fourteenth Amendment, 36

Fourth Amendment

dynamic entries violate, 79

militarization of police endangers, 74–75

racial profiling and, 124

Section 213 and, 97

Supreme Court decisions about, 97, 101, 118

violations, 37

free speech

barriers to exercise rights in, 39–40

Department of Justice does not protect, 35–39, 40–45

Free Trade Area of the Americas (FTAA) meeting, 41, 160

Frye, Marquette, 60

Fyfe, James, 83–84, 85

gay Americans, 53–54

Geneva Conventions, 89

ghettos, 59, 148

Goldberg, Jonah, 67

Guantánamo Bay detainees, 89

"Guidance Regarding the Use of Race by Federal Law Enforcement Agencies" (Department of Justice), 121–23, 125–26

Hames, Tim, 106

Hargrove, Simon, 14

Hayes, Anthony, 14

Hayward, John, 66

Hentoff, Nat, 94

Hillman, Theresa, 143

Hispanics, 57, 124, 128

see also racial profiling

hogtying, 138

homeland security responsibilities, 89, 152–53

Honberg, Ron, 84

hot spots, 151

"How to Train Cops" (Mac Donald), 31–32

Hulnick, Arthur, 90

Human Rights Watch, 15

internal controls

vs. external, 32–33

weakness of, 61–62

Johnston, Thomas E., 103

Jones, Nathaniel, 48–49

Jones, Prince, 24
Jones, Thomas, 23

Kelling, George, 149
Kerner Commission, 60
killing. *See* murder
King, Rodney, 19–20, 60, 156
Korematsu v. United States, 124

Latinos, 57, 124, 128
  see also racial profiling
Law Enforcement Education Program (LEEP), 148
Lawrenceville, Georgia, 23
Lee, Wen Ho, 23
lesbian Americans, 53–54
Levi, Edward, 40
Levy, Robert A., 130
LGBT Americans, 53–54
Livingstone, Ken, 107
London (England), 107–10, 112, 113, 114
Los Angeles Police Department (LAPD)
  evidence planted by, 23
  excessive force used by, 19–20, 53, 60, 78
  oversight of, 43
  racial profiling charges against, 128–32
Louima, Abner, 22
Lund, Nelson, 120
lynchings, 58–59

Mac Donald, Heather, 31–32, 63, 127
magic lanterns, 94
Maryland, 24, 82, 151
mass arrests, 19
McDuffie, Arthur, 60
McLaughlin, Carl, 64, 65

media
  ignores views of black police officers, 68
  independent, 156–62
  presents distorted portrayal of police, 30
Meiklejohn, Alexander, 36
Memphis, Tennessee, 84
Menezes, Jean Charles de, 107
mentally ill, 82–86, 136, 137–38
Miami Police Department, 41, 60
militarization
  communities of color become occupied areas, 59
  increases use of excessive force, 71–72
  of Miami Police Department, 41
  of search and seizure practices, 75–80
  SWAT teams and, 73–74
  threatens Constitutional rights, 74–75
  war on terrorism has increased, 50
"Militarization" (Dunn), 72
Minneapolis Police Department, 78
Minnesota, University of, 145
Miranda v. Arizona, 75, 118
misconduct, 16, 56
  discipline of
    can be effective, 25–26, 32–33
    is rare, 37, 61–62
  against LGBT Americans, 53–54
  oversight of, 43–45
  sneak and peek searches provide limitless opportunities for, 96, 97–98
  Supreme Court decisions about, 118–19
  see also force, excessive
Mises, Ludwig von, 47

Moore, Richard P., 92
Morais, Julio, 82
murder
    death penalty, 59–60
    justified, 47–48, 49
    lynchings, 58–59
    shoot-to-kill policies, 15, 107–10, 112–15
    targeted, 113

National Advisory Commission on Civil Disorders (1967), 60
National Lawyers Guild, 35
National Negro Congress (NNC), 61
Native Americans, 57
    see also racial profiling
neighborhood policing. See community policing programs
New Jersey state troopers, 22, 48
New Orleans Police Department (NOPD), 14–17
Newsday (newspaper), 75
News of the World (British newspaper), 109–10
Newsweek (magazine), 89
New York Police Department (NYPD)
    excessive use of force by
        decrease in, 25
        examples of, 22–23, 53, 60, 71–72, 82, 85
        training of, 32
    war on terrorism and, 42
Nickerson, Michael, 82, 86
Nickerson, Sue, 82, 85–86
no fly lists, 42
no-knock search warrants, 96–97
    see also sneak and peek searches

One Hundred Blacks in Law Enforcement Who Care, 67

Orange County (California), 145
Ottolenghi, Emanuele, 111

PATRIOT Act (2001 and 2006). See USA PATRIOT Act (2001 and 2006)
Philadelphia Police Department, 23, 82
Pittsburgh Police Department, 43, 44
police departments. See specific cities or counties
police dogs, 19
post-traumatic stress disorder, 15
Pratt, Desmond, 15
Pratt, Jonie, 15
Prince George's County (Maryland), 24
prison system, mentally ill in, 83
privacy, loss of, 94–95
problem-oriented policing. See community policing programs
protesters
    are spied on, 38, 40–42
    civil rights, 19
    Department of Justice encourages police abuse of, 35–39, 40–45
    use of excessive force against, 39
    videotaping can protect, 160
public opinion
    about racial profiling, 121
    supports expression of unpopular ideas, 36–37
    videotaping helps shape, 157–58

al Qaeda detainees, 89
qualified immunity, 118–19

racial profiling
    effects on people of color, 26

extent of, is exaggerated, 30–31
incidents of, 14–15, 22–24
is accepted police procedure, 48
is ineffective method of law enforcement, 33
is myth, 66
by LAPD, 128–32
Supreme Court decisions about, 124, 130
war on terrorism and, 121–26
racism
charges of, are political, 64
death penalty and, 59–60
is ingrained in American society, 56–59
police fear charge of, 67
use of excessive force and, 14–15
see also racial profiling
Redenbaugh, Russell, 28
Rehnquist, William H., 118
Revolutionary Worker (magazine), 26, 48, 75
Riley, Warren, 14–15
Rinaldo, Rachel, 160
Rivera, Belica, 75
Riveria, Lino, 60
roadblocks, 50
Roberts, John G., 119
Rockwell, Llewellyn H., Jr., 46
Rogers, Susan, 82–85
Rosenberg, Chuck, 99
rules of proportionality, 49–50

San Antonio Police Department, 53
San Diego Law Review (journal), 97
Saucier v. Katz, 118–19
Scahill, Jeremy, 41
Schneier, Bruce, 108

search and seizure practices
militarization of, 75–80
warrants
Alito decisions about, 119
conventional, 93–94, 100–101
no-knock, 96–97
Supreme Court decisions about, 97, 101, 118
USA PATRIOT Act and, 92–93, 94–95, 97–98, 100–103, 104–105
see also sneak and peek searches
Seattle Police Department, 142
Section 213 (USA PATRIOT Act), 92–93, 94–95, 97–98, 100–103, 104–105
sexual orientation, 53–54
shoot-to-kill policies, 15, 107–10, 112–15
slavery, 58
Smith, Rick, 139
Smith, Troy, 66
Smith, William French, 40
sneak and peek searches
names for, 93, 94
provide limitless opportunities for misconduct, 96, 97–98
Supreme Court decisions about, 97, 101
under USA PATRIOT Act, 92–93, 94–95, 97–98, 100–103, 104–105
use of, 104–105
sniffer keystroke loggers, 94
society
capitalist, results in police abuses, 26
LGBT community and, 53–54
police reflect norms of, 31, 67
racism is ingrained in, 56–60

videotaping is tool for watching agents of, 157–58
soldiers, police as. See militarization
special prosecutors, 32
Spruill, Alberta, 71–72, 75
spying, domestic, 38, 40–42
Stamper, Norman, 39
Stanford Law Review (journal), 98
Steubenville (Ohio) Police Department, 43
Stevens, Sir John, 109–10
Stonewalled—Still Demanding Respect (Amnesty International), 53–54
stop-and-frisk tactics, 26–27
strict scrutiny test, 122–23
Studdard, Marshall Dwight, 23
stun grenades, 76–80
stun guns, 134–38, 140–45, 156
suicide by cop, 143
Summit of the Americas, 41, 160
Supreme Court
    police misconduct decisions by, 118–19
    racial profiling decisions by, 124, 130
    sneak and peek searches decisions by, 97, 101
surreptitious entry searches. See sneak and peek searches
SWAT teams, 73–74

"Taking Liberty with Freedom" (Moore), 92
Taliban detainees, 89
targeted killings, 113
Taser International, 140
tasers, 134–38, 140–45, 156
terrorism. See war on terrorism
Tieger, Alan, 20
Timoney, John, 41

training
    dealing with mentally ill and, 83, 84
    use of force and, 14–15, 25–26, 31–32
    videotaping as tool for, 161
transgendered Americans, 53–54
transparency of police, 162

United Nations (UN), 136–37, 141–42
USA PATRIOT Act (2001 and 2006)
    protesters are spied on under, 38, 40–42
    provisions, 89, 92
    search warrants and, 92–93, 94–95, 97–98, 100–103, 104–105

videotaping, 156–62
    by law enforcement, 41
    use of excessive force and, 19–20, 23
Violent Crime Control and Law Enforcement Act (1994), 62

Waldman, Adelle, 81
Wall Street Journal (newspaper), 159–60
war on drugs, 103–104
war on terrorism
    dissenters are targeted as enemies, 36, 38
    domestic spying by FBI and, 38, 40–42
    has increased use of excessive force, 50
    homeland security as primary law enforcement focus, 89, 152–53
    needs must balance civil rights, 115
    racial profiling and, 121–26

requires sneak and peek
searches, 100, 103
shoot-to-kill policies and,
107–10, 112–15
see also USA PATRIOT Act
(2001 and 2006)
*Warrior Cops: The Ominous
Growth of Paramilitarism in
American Police Departments*
(Weber), 72–75
warrior police self-image, 74
Weber, Diane Cecilia, 72–75, 80
Welch, Ed, 143

Who Is Guarding the Guardians?
(U.S. Commission on Civil
Rights), 21, 29
Wilkes, Donald E., Jr., 70, 91
Williams, Hubert, 32–33
Wilson, James Q., 149
Wisler, Dominique, 155
World Trade Organization
(WTO), 39
World War II, 124

Zito, Frank, 86